Quarterly Essay

CONTENTS

Quarterly Essay is published four times a year by Black Inc., an imprint of Schwartz Publishing Pty Ltd
Publisher: Morry Schwartz

ISBN 186 395 3418
ISSN 1832-0953

Subscriptions (4 issues): $49 a year within Australia incl. GST (Institutional subs. $59). Outside Australia $79. Payment may be made by Mastercard, Visa or Bankcard, or by cheque made out to Schwartz Publishing. Payment includes postage and handling.

To subscribe, fill out and post the subscription form on the last page of this essay, or subscribe online at:

www.quarterlyessay.com

Correspondence and subscriptions should be addressed to the Editor at:

Black Inc.
Level 5, 289 Flinders Lane
Melbourne VIC 3000 Australia
Phone: 61 3 9654 2000
Fax: 61 3 9654 2290
Email: quarterlyessay@blackincbooks.com
http://www.quarterlyessay.com

Editor: Chris Feik
Management: Sophy Williams
Production Co-ordinator: Caitlin Yates
Publicity: Meredith Kelly
Design: Guy Mirabella

INTRODUCTION

Until recently I knew only as much or as little about the Family Court as anyone who follows current affairs. Two or three years ago I was sufficiently disturbed by what I was learning to open a newspaper cuttings file: this signals that the subject may be one on which I write "someday". Last year, suddenly, I was in the Family Court. I was not a principal in the case; I was appointed by the Court to supervise Steve, a student of mine, when he saw his children. His wife claimed he was a danger to them. My job was to watch him closely and to end the access and remove the children if danger loomed.

The visits lasted two hours on a Saturday morning and took place at an outer suburban McDonald's. Within half an hour of our first visit, I knew that my responsibilities would be light. Steve played exuberantly and imaginatively with his boys, who were plainly delighted to be with him. He wiped noses, changed nappies and settled disputes with a practised hand.

For six months I lived close to a man who had the common experience in divorce of being brought under suspicion and having to prove himself innocent. The day Steve was told of his wife's accusations was the day I determined that I must write about this Court. I have now studied the Court intensively and this essay is the outcome. I am grateful to Black Inc. for allowing it to be part of their *Quarterly Essay* series.

The system I describe here, or at least some part of it, may soon be modified. After the most recent parliamentary review of the Family Court, the Commonwealth government has decided to implement what it hopes will be significant changes. There have been earlier attempts to change the Family Court, which the Court has ignored or frustrated. The account that I offer of how this occurred should assist those attempting the latest reform. I will assess the government's reform plans at the end of the essay.

For the last fifteen years the Court has been symbolised by its chief justice, Alastair Nicholson, who retired in 2004. He was highly ambitious for his Court, ferocious in its defence and scathing of its critics. Much of the essay is an argument with him. He was appointed by the Hawke Labor government, but Labor as well as Coalition MPs became highly critical of him. He in turn did not hide his contempt for the politicians. He has been replaced as chief justice by Diana Bryant who is much quieter and conciliatory. It is too early to say whether she will change the outlook and practice of the Court.

The *Family Law Act* prohibits the discussion of its cases in a way that would reveal the identity of the people concerned. The names of the people I have interviewed have accordingly been changed. I am very grateful to Paul Walton, Graham Sweetland and Julian Aston who have allowed me to make public their experiences and their views of the Court.

The essay has benefited from the critical reading of Robert Manne and George Winterton. Jeremy Sammut has been more than a research assistant; he has been a keen collaborator. My thanks to them.

John Hirst

"KANGAROO COURT"	Family Law in Australia

John Hirst

I am writing to voice my disgust as to my treatment by your Kangaroo Court known as the Family Court. – *Submission no. 68 to the 1992 Select Committee on the Family Law*

THE CARING COURT

One of the gravest failings of the Family Court derives from the noble intentions of its founders.

The *Family Law Act* of 1975 which established the Court was a progressive social reform of the Whitlam Labor government. It was not an exclusively government measure; members on both sides were allowed a free vote and Liberals had been among those working for divorce law reform. The Act removed fault as a ground for divorce and replaced it with irretrievable breakdown, to be indicated by a one-year separation.

The aim was to allow couples to part without the trauma and contrivance of one partner proving fault against the other. Marriages would be buried decently and humanely. The business of dividing property, arranging maintenance and determining custody of children would remain, but these were to be settled in a simple, flexible and inexpensive way. Litigation was to be discouraged and the Court was to be staffed by social workers and counsellors as well as judges. It was to be a court of an entirely new sort, a "caring court" or a "helping court".

If proceedings were to be simple, flexible and cheap, why, say the wits, were lawyers put in charge of them? Proceedings quickly became complex, rule-bound and expensive – which was not entirely the fault of the lawyers because property settlements and custody cases can be very complex. But though the "caring court" looked more and more like an ordinary court, it hesitated to act like an ordinary court when its orders were disobeyed.

The disobeying of a court order is known as contempt of court and is the offence that threatens the foundations of our society. We are governed by the rule of law and once courts have settled the law, it has to be obeyed by governments and citizens alike. To ensure that their orders are obeyed, courts have large, discretionary powers to fine and imprison those who defy them. Though it was to be a court of a new sort, the Family Court had been equipped with these powers.

Within months of the Court opening, a Family Court judge used these powers to deal with a man who had defied a court order. His offence was indeed gross. His former wife had custody of their children and since he had been violent towards her, he had been put under a restraining order. One day he burst into her house unannounced, waving a gun, and threatened to kill his son if he did not come with him. The judge sent him to prison for twenty-eight days. From his prison cell, he appealed to the Full Family Court to release him.

The Full Court under the leadership of its first chief, Elizabeth Evatt, was embarrassed at their new "caring court" acting in this crude, old-fashioned way. It immediately set down for itself rules to limit the powers it had been given to punish contempt. An offender had to be properly tried for the contempt, and imprisonment was to be used only as a last resort; counselling, fines and recognisances should be considered first. In the case before them, the appeal judges were disturbed at the trial judge opting immediately for imprisonment, which seemed the more unnecessary since the offender was to face charges in a criminal court, which could well result in a gaol sentence. They released the man from gaol. (The trial judge had been well aware that the offender was facing criminal charges; he reasoned that since the man was still at large he needed to be taught a lesson immediately so that his former wife might feel safe.)

However, the Court quickly became much more hard-headed, as it regularly had to deal with cases of men abducting children from their mothers. The offenders were given gaol sentences. The Court declared that though it was a helping court, its orders had to be obeyed. "Others who may contemplate disobedience of the Court need to know that calculated and grave contempt of its orders will not be tolerated."

One abduction case, G and G (1981), was of great significance. A father had abducted his son from the mother and lived with him for four years before they were discovered. The man was sent to gaol for two and a half years for defying the Court's orders. His offence was that he had isolated his son from his mother, but was the Court now going to damage the boy further by depriving him of his father, with whom he got on well? The judge gave the matter earnest consideration because judges are charged under the Family Law Act to give paramount consideration to the welfare of the child. The judge decided that "in a contempt matter the welfare of the child is not the paramount consideration, though it is a matter that must be considered". This approach was upheld by the Full Court when the father appealed against his imprisonment. Chief Judge Evatt, conceding that the imprisonment of the father may cause suffering to the child, nevertheless said: "If no punishment is imposed, or if lenience is shown, the court's power to protect not only the individual child concerned, but also many other children, may be diminished."

These hard-headed pronouncements were all made in cases where fathers did not have custody of their children and had taken matters into their own hands. When the Court came to consider breaches of orders by custodial parents (chiefly mothers), it returned to soft-headedness. The typical case was where a mother contrived to deny a father access to his children, even though he had court orders allowing access (usually it is for every second weekend and half the school holidays). In considering its response to such breaches, the Court declared that the paramount interests of *this particular child* must prevail. Since the Court could scarcely fine or imprison a custodial mother without having some effect on the child, these options were effectively abandoned. So the "caring court" re-emerged.

The Court was not impelled to this decision by the *Family Law Act*, which gave untrammelled power to punish for contempt, and in adopting it the Court ignored its own judgements in the abduction cases. Just as the Court had there imagined, leniency had disastrous consequences for children. Since access orders were defied with impunity, thousands of children were kept from their fathers, though the Court had ruled that their best interests required that they see them.

Mothers contrive to deny access to fathers by being away when the father calls, or claiming that the child is ill or does not want to go, or alleging that the father is mistreating the child – or simply moving to a new location. Mothers frequently have good reason to fear access: violent fathers use the contact to re-open old quarrels, to attack the mother and unsettle the children. The Court allows that the custodial parent can deny access with reasonable excuse. If the father is violent, the mother can ask the Court to vary its order and deny him access. If the Court allows access to continue, the pick-up point will be a supervised contact centre where the man will not see his ex-wife. But mothers are not simply keeping away unsatisfactory fathers; decent fathers are being denied access to their children. Mothers who have nothing more to fear from the Court than a slap on the wrist, can, if they wish, exclude fathers from their children's lives.

The Court itself is not in any matter responsible for enforcing its orders. A father who is denied access must bring action in the Court and either bear the costs of a lawyer ($3000 a day minimum) or conduct the case himself. But even if he wins the case, the mother will not suffer a penalty that will deter her. When the next contact visit falls due, she may well behave in exactly the same way. The Court has made clear in its judgements that the custodial parent is not to be the judge of whether contact is beneficial. However, by making the best interests of the particular child the test when enforcement is being considered, the Court has given the custodial parent de facto control over access.

So the logic of the Family Court is as follows:

The best interests of the child require that they have contact with both parents.

However, if the custodial parent is determined to deny access to the other parent,

Then the best interests of the child require that the child have contact with only one parent.

Of course one would prefer that a custodial parent did not have to be coerced into providing access. But if the custodial parent is to determine the matter, why have a court at all? This is not to suggest that the best interests of the child should be overlooked in enforcement; rather that they should not be the paramount consideration – which is what the Court accepted in G and G. The paramount consideration when the Court has been deliberately and persistently defied must be the upholding of the authority of the Court.

The constant refrain of the recently retired Chief Justice of the Court, Alastair Nicholson, was that you cannot fine a custodial mother or put her in gaol. Other jurisdictions do not accept this limitation. A single mother has to pay fines for parking and traffic offences, and many women in gaol are mothers. A single mother who cheats the social security system may occasionally be put in gaol, a necessary act to preserve the integrity of the system. The Family Court has no understanding of system integrity.

But why the talk of gaol? You may think that milder penalties consistently enforced would prove effective. You may think this, but the Family Court, as we will see later, has not been interested in that approach either.

Family Court judges expatiate on the dilemma they face over enforcement since theirs is a "caring court", which puts the interests of the child first. A caring court! It has not cared for the thousands of non-custodial parents who have wasted their spirit and resources, not in attempting to overturn a decision of the Court, but in a futile attempt to get the Court to enforce its own orders so that they might see their children. Thousands more, perhaps wisely, have decided not to make the attempt. In *Middlemarch* George Eliot writes that if we could hear the pain of the ordinary tragedies of human life in our midst, the sound would deafen us. When Family Court judges talk piously of the "caring court", I wish they could hear the roar of pain that their piety has caused.

The man who called the Family Court a "kangaroo court" in his submission to the 1992 parliamentary enquiry claimed he had spent $15,000 in a futile attempt to get access to his children. His former wife simply refused to open the door when he called to collect them.

> To my utter disgust and dismay the Family Court judge decided that while I had done all I could as a father, he was powerless to enforce access if she refused to open the door. He just laughed and said "SEND THEM A CHRISTMAS CARD AND SEE WHAT HAPPENS".

Is this credible? A report of the Law Reform Commission does record this view of one judge: "I am very slow to attach *any sanctions at all* to breaches of access orders."

The other systematic failure in enforcement was the Court's inability to compel non-custodial parents (chiefly fathers) to pay maintenance for the support of their children. Only about 30 to 40 per cent did so. It was in this way that custodial mothers suffered from the laxity of the Court. The low rate of maintenance payment greatly concerned the Treasury because separated mothers were drawing heavily on social security for their support. Indeed, in the heady days when welfare flowed freely, the Court organised the payment of maintenance so that it would not reduce the entitlement of custodial parents to social security. The government called a halt to this in 1988 when it established the Child Support Agency. The Agency collected funds from non-custodial parents and passed them to custodial parents.

The Child Support Agency is not a caring agency. It is ruthless and relentless; it deducts payments from wages and sweeps bank accounts. Its reputation is so fierce that people making payments outside the system are more likely to maintain them for fear of falling into its clutches. Unlike the Family Court, which has abandoned moral judgement for "no-fault", the Child Support Agency proclaims the moral principle that parents should pay for the upbringing of their children. In this way it has raised the rate of compliance to over 60 per cent.

The comparative success of the Agency means that many fathers who are not able to see their children are nevertheless paying to support them. Fathers' groups have proposed that fathers denied access should not have to pay maintenance. Policy-makers have looked at this option not unsympathetically, but the decision always is that access and maintenance should not be linked. The argument is that it is not in the best interests of the child to punish mothers by reducing their income. This is typical of thinking in family law matters. Everywhere else carrots and sticks work to keep us in order, but in the semi-chaotic world of the family law they are not to be contemplated. The picture is of thousands of children suffering economic deprivation. No one considers that a mother, motivated by care for her children, might well rethink her position on access in order to retain the maintenance. And if she didn't, the social security safety net does not allow anyone to fall into life-threatening hardship.

If maintenance and access were linked, there is a concern that fathers could avoid paying maintenance by abandoning their right of access. That could not be allowed. It would, however, be proper to say to a father that he would lose the right of access if maintenance were not paid.

The imbalance that has entered the system (as between enforcing maintenance and access) would be corrected if there were an Access Compliance Agency which would take responsibility for securing access where it had been unreasonably denied. This would remove from the access parent the cost and burden of running their own cases. Such a scheme has been proposed several times, but so far has not been implemented. In a 1998 study, the Family Law Council (a government-funded body established to research and report on the operation of family law) was surprised to find that in New Zealand if a custodial parent was refusing to grant access, a warrant was issued to take the child. Children were being forcibly removed! But it discovered further that once custodial parents received a warrant, nearly all of them voluntarily complied and allowed the child to go to the other parent. Since people knew that force would be used, force rarely had to be used. Such a beneficial calculus has not been allowed to operate under Australian family law. The Family Law Council thought something along New Zealand lines might be tried.

The establishment of the Child Support Agency and the proposal for an Access Compliance Agency are clear signs that the Family Court is a failing institution. Since it can't or won't do its job, it is being bypassed. In 1999 the government established the Federal Magistrates Court and gave it family law among its jurisdictions in the hope that some cases might be resolved simply and cheaply – which, of course, is what the Family Court was meant to do.

The Family Court has defended its poor record on enforcement by highlighting the difficulties it faces. Cases in other civil courts are settled by a single transaction. By contrast, a single order from the Family Court refers to innumerable transactions, for example a father is to have access to his children every second weekend. On each access visit there is occasion for a breach of the order, many of a trivial kind. The mother may not have the children ready at the appointed time; a father might bring the children back late. It would be a mistake to take all these alleged breaches seriously. Where parents are still at war or are mentally unstable, the whole business of contact is terribly fraught and is not likely to be solved by punishing one or other parent for breach of an order.

No one doubts the difficulties, but every enquiry into the Court's record has found that the Court has not made a concerted attempt to solve them. From its inception there have been regular enquiries into the Court's enforcement procedures. Parliamentary committees have reported in 1980, 1992 and 2003. There have been enquiries and critiques from the Law Council of Australia, the Police Commissioners of the states, the Australian Law Reform Commission and the Family Law Council. The following give the flavour of these reports:

1980 Law Council of Australia
Enforcement of contact orders is poor "not from lack of power under the Act, but rather from lack of implementation".

1985 Law Reform Commission
The Family Court presents "a unique result within contempt law and practice: namely that a court is consciously shying away from imposing penal sanctions on those who deliberately refuse or fail to obey its order".

1992 Parliamentary Committee
The Chief Justice should issue a directive to the judges informing them that (a) penalties for non-compliance of orders are contained in the Family Law Act (b) such penalties should be used in appropriate cases (c) such penalties should be consistently applied throughout the Family Court.

1998 Family Law Council
There is "a fairly widely held view in the community that the Family

Court is reluctant to enforce its own orders". Orders should carry a warning about the serious consequences of breaching an order. Judges should be directed in the *Family Law Act* that they must treat breaches of orders seriously.

None of these bodies was in favour of sharp punitive methods, that is, to lock up a few offenders in the hope that the rest would fall into line. They wanted the Court to use a range of remedies, but still keeping fines and imprisonment as the last resort. Above all they pleaded with the Court to take enforcement seriously; to be firm and consistent. None of them queried directly, as I have done here, the Court's doctrine that the best interests of the particular child must be paramount in the imposition of penalty. While that remains in place, firm action will prove difficult.

However, even on its own test that the interests of the particular child are paramount in all circumstances, the Court could have been acting differently if it thought of *long-term* interests. By not pressuring a mother who is unco-operative about access, the Court has left large numbers of children without an effective father. We are now more aware of the need of children, especially of boys, for a male role model; we are talking of mentors where there could have been fathers.

Twice parliament has attempted to guide the Court on how to proceed on enforcement. It has added new punishments (like community service orders and periodic detention) and structured penalties in rising levels of severity. The Court has not accepted this guidance. Parliament's last attempt was made in 2000. On that occasion Chief Justice Nicholson declared publicly that its measures would not work and accused the politicians of contributing to the problem by their criticisms of the Court: "the politicians who so readily attach themselves to concern about matters of compliance with orders ... might be well advised to reflect upon how their other comments and actions work against the adherence they purport to want to see." Though critical of parliament's measures he made no counter proposals, contenting himself with a rehearsal of all the difficulties the

Court faced. He reiterated his view that fines and imprisonment were "inappropriate" or "useless". So by signalling that the ultimate penalty was not to be invoked, the Chief Justice removed the inducement to take the lesser penalties seriously.

This is an amazing saga. For twenty-five years, the parliament and responsible public bodies have been concerned about the authority of the Court, and the Court itself has not. Everyone knows that Family Court orders are a joke, but the judges soberly continue to produce more of them. To all appearances, Chief Justice Nicholson was less interested in ensuring that the orders of his court were obeyed than in enhancing the status, salaries and accommodation of its judges.

The Family Court condemns itself. If its orders have been conscientiously framed to advance the best interests of children, then by its failure to enforce its orders it has been systematically damaging the children under its care.

PAUL WALTON

Of all the cases that go to the Family Court, only 5 per cent reach trial. The rest are resolved through mediation or agreement among the parties and the lawyers.

Sometimes defenders of the Court cite the low 5 per cent trial figure to show that most people are satisfied with how their cases are settled. This is far from the truth. People settle because they run out of money to pay lawyers (and haven't got the time and energy to conduct their own case) or they face an allegation that is too hard to fight or they are told they have no hope of winning what they might want. Fathers who want to see more of their children than every second weekend have little hope unless they can argue or allege that their wife is somehow unfit.

So the appetite and predilections of this legal monster control behaviour far from its lair. It is perfectly possible for a man to lose his children without stepping into the Court. Meet Paul Walton who can no longer see his children. He went to the Family Court only once over the custody of his children – to register the fact that he was abandoning his attempt to see them. He was very pleased with how he was treated.

Paul was a businessman and hopes to be so again. At the moment he is living in a tiny Housing Commission flat. When he and his wife separated, he gave her the house because he said he could quickly make enough money to buy one for himself. That hasn't happened yet – fighting for his kids has been his occupation for three years.

Paul ran the sort of businesses that can be conducted from home. For many years he was, in the Family Court's term, the primary carer of their two daughters while his wife pursued her career. He is a mild, quiet man who tells of his descent into the abyss in a monotone.

Like many others, he wants me to know how well regarded he was in his previous life. He was president of both the local Rotary Club and the Small Business Council. He did deals on a handshake. *No need to sign a contract with Paul Walton.* When he was selling insurance, he sold five policies on five contracts though they could have been accommodated on two. That increased his sales score. He couldn't live with himself. He went back two days later and redid the paperwork.

When Paul and his wife agreed to separate, they consulted a child psychologist on how best to prepare their daughters, aged thirteen and ten. The psychologist suggested that Paul acquire his own unit or flat before they told the children and have it set up as a place they could visit. They could then say immediately to them, "Come and look at Dad's house which will be your house too." This they did. The children were to have dinner with Paul every Tuesday and Thursday night and stay over every second weekend and for half the holidays.

Three days into the first holiday period Paul and his teenage daughter had an argument. She rang her mother and demanded to be taken home. The mother collected the girl and her sister. She insisted that in future if Paul saw the children she had to be present. He saw them a few times briefly, but visits with the wife present were not satisfactory. The visits tailed off.

Paul let matters ride, hoping the mother would come round. *I guess I was too soft, John. I ought to have put my foot down and said if you are not prepared to stick to the original agreement we must get it set out in court.* The reason he did not go to court was that friends who had been there warned him that the Court would eat up his money and perhaps still not give him the result he wanted.

Paul wrote letters to his wife and children pleading for the agreed arrangement to be re-established, with no result. So finally through legal aid he got a lawyer, who commenced proceedings by sending the wife a letter. *This letter sparked something really surprising.* The wife accused him of being "verbally abusive and physically intimidating". The children wrote in their own hand to say, "You are not our Dad and we don't want anything to do with you."

Now the man is as mild as Sandy Stone, but I know in domestic matters one can never tell. So I add the wife's testimony of a few years before, words inscribed in the front of a photo album that was a birthday present to her husband. Paul brought the album out not to show me this, but photos of his girls. The wife wrote: "What a blessing for the girls to have a father who tells stories, makes cubbies, catches bugs, teaches and listens. Listens and listens. What a blessing for me to have a husband who leads this family with love, devotion and gentleness."

Paul consulted a child psychologist on how he should respond. He told him: "At best after a long court hearing the younger daughter will be directed to have contact with you, but not overnight because you are now in a one-bedroom place. The older girl can refuse. It is likely that when you turn up to collect your girl, she will not be there. You will have to get another court order. You will collect her from the steps of a police station. Is that what you want?"

He did not want that.

A few months later he made another attempt to bring the wife to negotiation. A solicitor's letter came back referring to "a long, detailed and disturbing history about the difficulties over the years which are relevant to contact". He was being set up as mentally unstable. Paul has long had a bi-polar disorder that has been controlled by medication. The solicitor said should the matter go to court they would subpoena his various psychiatrists, psychologists and doctors to produce evidence of his medical history. Paul asked his present doctor how this would play out in court. His doctor assured him that he was perfectly stable and he would be happy so to testify. However, the other side could indeed subpoena all his medical records and quote selectively from them. He would then have to bring his previous doctors from interstate and have them testify on his behalf — to give a complete and not a partial account of his condition. The costs would be huge. It would be a battle royal from which the only winners would be the lawyers. Paul did not have the funds for this and Legal Aid would not assist.

Paul's various advisers knew the Family Court and its methods very well. He still kept out of it.

Paul realised that his greatest difficulty was that his wife was poisoning the girls against him. This practice has received a name: the Parent Alienation Syndrome. The concept has not gone unchallenged. Perhaps the children are not so much brainwashed by the custodial parent; they adopt their hostile views themselves, which is perfectly plausible given their eagerness to identify with the person caring for them. But either way they repeat the objections of their carer parent against the absent parent; they "sound very rehearsed, wooden, brittle and frequently use adult words and phrases". They take great delight in being hostile and rude to the parent with whom they used to be close.

Paul's last play was to suggest to his wife that he might have the Family Court make an assessment of her and her relations with the children. *The next day I received a phone call from my little one which frightened the heck out of me … She phoned me and swore like a trooper, telling me to fuck off for what I was doing to her and her family.* That was the end.

He does not expect to see his children again. *They're gone. They have been stolen. The Court could not help me. A guy feels totally impotent.* He saw his younger daughter for the last time ten months ago at her school break-up to which he was invited by the school. *I was sitting at the end of an aisle. First up were the grade sixers. Because her name is Walton, she was near the end of the queue. I am looking at this child. I had not seen her for eight months and that was only for half an hour at McDonald's for her birthday with her mother present. I looked at this girl again. She was a lot taller than I remembered; her hair was different and she was thinner in the face. That is my Christina. I tapped her on the shoulder just to say Hi. To let her know I was there. She turned away. She did not say Hello.* In documents submitted to the Court the mother objected to his coming unannounced to the school and harassing his daughter.

He and his former wife attended the Court to negotiate the terms on which she would send to him reports of the girls' activities. This is a standard Family Court procedure: the excluded parent indicates that they will abandon attempts to see their child in return for receiving news of them. Paul wanted these reports to come monthly; his former wife wanted them to be every three months. With the help of the Family Court coun-sellor they compromised on two months. *The counsellor was excellent. She jumped on both of us if we got out of line. She was quite impartial.*

Paul has received two reports and has decided that they are almost not worth having. They come as a grid with topics listed in one box and the briefest of answers in another. Paul's were the first of these reports that I had seen. I could scarcely believe that they existed. To get this infor-mation a parent signs away the right to see their children – what a confession of failure by the Court! This man lives in the same suburb as his children; he has committed no offence – and this is all the Family Court can offer him.

You are flying home from interstate late on a Friday afternoon. You strike up a conversation with the man next to you who says he's been away for three weeks and is looking forward to seeing his kids. Of all the things you might then say, you would never say this: Do you want to see your kids for their benefit or your own? This is the question the Family Court sometimes asks of non-custodial parents (mostly fathers) in its purist pursuit of the "best interests of the child".

People do not produce children for "the best interests of the child". We speak of a couple deciding to *have* children or not to *have* them. Very properly parents invest something of themselves in their child – without that investment their care and love would be less. Too much investment of course can be damaging – we speak of parents who are overly possessive. But we allow that parents can be proud of their children – or ashamed of them.

When we think of families, we do not consider whether the parents children have are in their best interests. We have decided that where parents are positively harmful they have to be controlled or the child removed and placed elsewhere, but we go no further. We do not interfere when a father persuades his son to abandon his homework and go fishing with him. Nor when a mother thinks she knows best whom her daughter should marry. There is no point in asking whether my children would have turned out better if I had not been an academic. Or whether Alastair Nicholson's children would have turned out better if he had not been a lawyer. Family is fate. This is something that cannot be unpicked.

The Family Court could have decided that when parents separate, children should continue to have contact with both parents unless they would do them harm – that is, the same standard we apply to intact families. It has rejected that view and insists that there is no presumptive right in a parent to see a child. The Court will decide in its judgement whether it is in the best interests of the child for the parent to see them. In the leading case on this matter, *Brown and Pedersen* (1992), the judges said, "This Court has long laid to rest any notion that a parent has a right to access." The Court may decide to grant access, but "until such order is made, no 'right of access' exists." The principle on which the Court operates is, "access by a non-custodial parent will only be ordered where access will advance and promote the welfare of the child."

The High Court has endorsed this approach. So for the moment this is the law of the land, made by judges and not the parliament. I trust that if the parliament were to consider the matter it would make the law differently.

It took some time for the Family Court to reach this definite view and there have been dissenters on the bench. Justice Kay gave a powerful dissenting judgement in an appeal case when two of his colleagues decided to uphold a decision to deny a father even supervised access to his child. The trial judge had said that access would not benefit the child and that he doubted whether it would be of much benefit to the father! Justice Kay said that the father clearly thought differently, for that was what he was applying for. He considered that the Court should be very reluctant to deny a parent access to a child and he refused to join his brethren in taking nothing for granted and assessing each access case on whether it was of benefit to the child:

> No relationship short of husband and wife is viewed by the law as
> important as that of parent and child. In my view it is unnecessary
> in the vast majority of access cases to have to prove that the contin-
> uance of the parent–child relationship will be to the child's benefit.
> It goes without saying.

He read into his judgement quotations from the literature on children and divorce to show that the mental health of children is threatened if they lose contact with a parent after divorce.

Why did the Court move to its purist position? Perhaps they were driven there by the *Family Law Act*, which does declare that in making its judgements the Court must treat children's interests as paramount. However, paramount does not mean that all other considerations are to be ignored. An early judgement in *Cooper* (1977), which the Court has now repudiated, acknowledged that the child's interests were paramount but declared, "the interests of the parent seeking access are relevant and are not to be ignored."

It may look at first sight as if the Court succumbed to the temptations of social engineering, thinking it could improve on nature and give children parents in the proportions that would most benefit them. Justice Nygh, in a case frequently cited (*Cotton*, 1983), did express himself in this way. He declared that the Court should assess the quality of a parent's relationship with the child and what they could offer:

> I can well imagine that in certain circumstances a woman who leads a totally immoral life such as a prostitute may have something to offer her children. On the other hand, it may be that a person who leads a life which to the general observer is one of a pillar of rectitude has nothing to offer to his children.

Who today would doubt the former proposition? Who, apart from a Family Court judge, would even entertain the latter? Fortunately this approach is not common. The Court does not generally operate with these standards of judgement: it gives custody to the parent who has been the primary carer unless they are clearly incapable and in most cases allows access to a non-custodial parent (though, as we have seen, it does not enforce its own access orders). It does, however, hold zealously to the principle that there is no presumption of access.

The reason for the Court's zealotry is not that it is too much the social engineer, but that it does not want to engineer enough. It usually allocates children to their mother, with the father having access, and no matter what the mother subsequently does it is reluctant to penalise the mother or disturb her custody of the children. A mother might turn a child so against their father that the child says they no longer want to see him. The Court will decide that it is no longer in the interests of the child to see the father, even though the father has done nothing wrong. A mother might fear that her child will be harmed by the father on access visits. The Court decides that there is no danger, but if the mother still genuinely believes that the child is in danger, the Court considers that an anxious mother will be a poorer parent and the child will suffer. Hence the father is not to see the child or to see the child only under supervision, even though he is innocent. The father in each case has been treated appallingly, which makes plain why the Court has to insist that there is no right of access. But since the Court has operated on the principle (narrowly conceived) that the child's interests are paramount, the judges sleep easily in their beds.

We should not underestimate the moral strain of being a Family Court judge. Not only do judges have to put aside all moral judgements concerning the break-up of the marriage, they have chosen to continue in moral suspense as they consider the behaviour of the divorced couple as it affects their children. As one respected judge put it, they must make their decisions in the sort of cases just discussed unmoved by "considerations of either sympathy for the innocent non-custodial parent or feelings of frustration or annoyance with the custodial parent". That is no doubt a strain, but they can point to the higher principle, which trumps all others, of the best interests of the child.

The early case of *Cooper*, in which Justice Samuels accepted that the parents had a legitimate interest in their children, was not decided in the Family Court. It was a left-over from the previous era and was a decision on appeal of the New South Wales Supreme Court, though it entered the law books of the new Court. It breathes an entirely different atmosphere from a Family Court case, more robust, less abject and more moral. Remember, though, this court was acting under the same principle of the best interests of the child, but rather differently conceived.

The judges ordered that the father in the case should have access to his two boys, though he was a man lacking "any settled purpose and unstable in character". The court said that those failings would tell against him if he were asking for custody, but since boys should know their fathers he should have access. The mother and her family were opposed to any further contact with the father. Recently the father had had access to his older boy, but at the home of his ex-wife and with her and her "army of relations" present. The visit had not gone well, but the judges discounted this. How could the boy engage with his father in the presence of all these people who were hostile to him? The court, with elaborate courtesy, said it was not suggesting that the mother and her family had deliberately set out to prejudice the boy against his father, but the boy must have been aware of their hostility. He had been placed in an impossible emotional position. In future the father and the boy should see each other alone. The man had never seen his younger son, but he was to have access to him as well.

The court had some sympathy for the mother, who had been given much grief by this man, but told her that she had to submerge her feelings and encourage a positive attitude in the boy towards his father. One judge, quoting an English judgement, told her that it was "the duty of parents ... to inculcate in the child a proper attitude of respect to the other parent". So this court told the mother that she had to change her ways; the Family Court would have yielded to her hostility and anxiety.

The approach of the Family Court can be summarised in this way. The Court encounters a broken family – the husband and wife have separated – and then it creates a second break between parent and child: it reduces parents to the status merely of candidates for involvement in their children's lives. It then re-assembles child and parents in the way it considers will best advance the interests of the child, but it does not enforce the orders that embody this settlement. A better approach would be (1) to acknowledge the strength of the bond between parent and child (2) to work for a settlement which as far as possible kept both parents involved in the lives of their children (so long as they would do them no harm) and (3) to take firm action against a parent who jeopardised this arrangement.

There would be nothing wrong with the Family Court taking the children's interest as paramount so long as it accepted the paradox that a recognition of the parents' interest in the child is the best way to secure the child's best interests. The best interests of the child, as currently interpreted by the Court, are a cover for its own timidity. Action of the sort contemplated in point (3) above is not its style.

Within the Court, but not on the bench, something like this alternative approach is already followed. In their mediation work, the Court's counsellors aim no higher than securing the least worst option for the child and, crucially, they work for a settlement which both parents can live with, seeing that as the best chance for a satisfactory life for the child. What a relief it is to read of this approach, in such contrast to the high-mindedness of the bench.

Imagine if the Court were more ordinary in its aims – and more ambitious – and it attempted to settle disputes as best it could according to the wishes and interests of all parties, mother, father and child. Then it might be troubled to discover that groups of fathers all round the country were critical of what the Court and the family law system had meted out to them. But a caring court that has put the interests of children first sees in its critics only people who don't share its own high ideals. When these fathers complained, Chief Justice Nicholson called on them to stop thinking of themselves and think of the children (whom by the action or inaction of his Court they might be unable to see). Recently the President of the Family Division of the English High Court has said the same: how can we be biased against fathers when we are putting the interests of the children first?

In the eyes of the Court and all those who accept its interpretation of the best interests of the child, non-custodial parents cease to be normal human beings with the expectations and limitations of our kind. They are persons from whom anything can be taken or of whom anything may be demanded, because all that is done is for the best interests of the children. We will follow this process by considering what may seem a minor matter – the names children bear after divorce – and the major matter of the payment of child support.

In our society it is still the norm for children to take their father's surname. We understand why a man wants a child (particularly a boy) to carry on his name. We take pleasure in seeing a son follow in his father's footsteps. When Don Bradman's son changed his name, we understand why he did so – and why his father was so hurt.

The Family Court pays no respect to the naming that links generations. When it decides on the names children will have after the divorce of their parents, it gives no weight to the wishes and what it dismissively calls the "proprietorial interests" of the parents. What is normal in the world at large becomes suspect in the Family Court. One judge, tiring of this part of his business, opined that parents in the Court attached far too much importance to the question of the child's surname. The judge, however, did not conclude his remarks by announcing that his own children were no longer to bear his name as an example of the proper attitude to this matter.

The Family Court has regularly to consider the naming of children because mothers who remarry or repartner change their children's name to that of their step-father. The law on this matter is clear: children's names can be changed only with the consent of both parents. Of course names can be changed informally: the mother simply enters her children at school under the new name. The Family Court rule on informal change of names is equally clear: it can only occur with the consent of both parents.

One might think, therefore, that the Court would have an easy task in dealing with this issue. Whenever a father complained that his name had been removed from his children without his consent, the Court would order its restoration. Having read this far, you will not be surprised to learn that this is not the approach of the Family Court. The Court considers whether keeping the new name or reverting to the old one will be in the best interests of the child. It has developed a list of considerations to guide its deliberations, among them the embarrassment to a child over its name or change of name, the child's sense of identity, the effect of naming on the child's relationship with parents, the inadvisability of frequent changes of name.

Here is an example of the Court at work on this issue. The judge is delivering his verdict in the case of *Garden v Garden* (1982). The former Mrs Garden had changed her children's names to Hawkins, the name of her new partner.

> There can be no doubt on the evidence before me that the wife enrolled the children at school and has generally adopted the name of Hawkins as their surname without any prior consultation with the husband whatsoever.
>
> The husband is in the Armed Forces and his service commitments render it impossible for him to have access to his children on a regular basis. Further, the wife is now living at the country town YY and the distance from the husband's regular work and his children has been a further impediment to access.
>
> Notwithstanding the problems enumerated above, the husband does have regular contact with his children and the wife in cross-examination admitted that both children had a good relationship with their father and that there existed a strong degree of loyalty towards him.
>
> The case put on behalf of the wife stated shortly is as follows:
> (a) That the children live in a small country town and it would save embarrassment for them if they were to take the name of the wife's present husband.
> (b) The husband does not live in the said town nor in close proximity to it and could not therefore be said to be affected by any change of name.
> The case for the husband on the other hand was put as follows:
> (a) That he has a strong relationship with both his children.
> (b) He desires that his children retain his name.
> (c) That the wife's attitude in changing the children's names was

made without his consent and to that extent was high-handed.

(d) That the embarrassment alleged is more in the minds of Mr and Mrs Hawkins than the children.

Evidence was given with regard to the wishes of the children particularly the wishes said to have been expressed by the son [who wanted to retain his father's name]. In my view, the children in this case have informed each parent what that parent wishes to hear. The children are no doubt aware that they are at the centre of the present dispute and I have no doubt that once a decision has been made it will be accepted by the children and enable the parties to settle down to a normal pattern of living.

I have had referred to me the various authorities in relation to the matter ... It is clear that the most important consideration is what is in the best interests of the children. Before determining this question, I must consider the short and long-term effects of any change in the children's surname as well as any embarrassment likely to be experienced by them if their name is different from that of the custodial parent.

I do not believe that the husband fully understands the embarrassment in which the wife now finds herself in endeavouring to bring up children with a surname different from her own. On the other hand, I do not think that the wife fully appreciates the husband's desire for the children to continue to bear his name.

There is no doubt upon the evidence before me that the Garden children are happy well-adjusted children who have settled into their new environment reasonably well. In addition, they have the advantage of a caring and concerned father who is obviously anxious to do what he can to assist in their upbringing and future development.

The judge then delivered judgement to the effect that the children should keep their new name, Hawkins, as a matter of common usage, including on school records, provided that the school documents also stated that their surname is Garden.

You will be struck by the fair-mindedness of the judge. Of course. The faults of the Family Court do not derive from a lack of judiciousness in the judges. Within the parameters they set themselves, they are conscientious. You may also agree that the judge's decision was in the best interests of the children. But now look at the father's experience of this transaction. He has discovered that his children's names have been changed without reference to him. He has spent money to take the case to court whereupon his wife's lawyer questions the strength of his ties with the children. Fortunately his own lawyer by cross-examination of the wife has revealed that he has a good relationship with his children. The judge has declared that he is a "caring and concerned father". The judge has also found that his wife changed the children's names without his consent and hence acted wrongly. But the father still loses the case. A bond with his children that he thought important has been broken without his consent and as a result of no wrong-doing on his part. His children now go under another name. This he has to bear in the best interests of the children.

How could it be different? If it were known that the Court always acted firmly to restore names, then it would be mothers who had to ponder more deeply the best interests of the children. If they changed names without the father's consent, they would most likely impose on the children the embarrassment and inconvenience of having them changed back. So most would obey the law and the rule of the Court.

One judge, upset at where the best interests of the child had led him in a name case (to rule against the father), suggested that when parents were granted a divorce, the papers should state clearly that names of children were not to be changed unilaterally. This was not taken up and it would have made no difference. The Court is committed to ignoring wrongful behaviour in a custodial parent unless it damages the best interests of the child. This makes it hard for non-custodial parents to see it as a court of justice.

That non-custodial parents should help support their children financially is a responsibility they usually accept, at least in principle. In practice fathers (who constitute 90 per cent of the payers) are full of complaints about how the child support system operates.

The payments they have to make are quite substantial. For one child the parent has to pay 18 per cent of their income, for two children 27 per cent, for three children 32 per cent. This is assessed on gross income, that is before tax, which means that the actual rates on take-home pay are much higher. However, to guarantee non-custodial parents enough money to live on, an amount slightly more than the base pension is excluded from the calculation. Those on salary and wages have their maintenance taken from their pay. Those who are self-employed can lower their incomes (as they do to evade or minimise tax) and hence their payment obligation. The Child Support Agency pursues them, makes an estimate of their true income and is employing ever more draconian measures to get money out of them for current obligations and debts.

Men on low incomes – which encompasses a high proportion of divorced fathers – struggle to meet these commitments. After the turmoil and expense of the divorce, they have to support children in their old home (which the wife usually retains) while they are attempting to establish a new one. But surely they can live cheaply in a small flat? No, because if they want to have the children stay overnight on access visits they will need bedrooms for them. And later they may repartner and again have a household of children. If they take on overtime and second jobs to cover all these expenses, they find that these are also taxed at the same rate.

Unwilling or unable to make their payments and pay back their debts, many men simply give up and go on the dole or if self-employed declare bankruptcy. The numbers are not known, but they are enough to register with members of parliament who get more complaints about family law and child support than any other matters. A select committee in 1992 declared, "Forcing people to leave their jobs or into bankruptcy is unconscionable," but the system remains basically unchanged. The government has an expert group examining it, which is to report in March 2005.

So far the government has driven the fathers hard because it wants to recoup some of the money it pays in welfare to their ex-wives. The great majority of separated wives and their children have very low incomes and are heavily reliant on welfare. To lower men's commitments would reduce the incomes of these households and children would be deprived. The government has been trying to square the circle. A man on a low income or even a middle-to-low income cannot live decently and at the same time make a substantial contribution to his former household. Either the government has to discourage divorce or bear more of its costs.

The system breeds resentment. A wife might remarry someone quite well off but her former husband has to keep paying maintenance at the same rate (the income of new partners is not taken into account at all). The wife herself might have a reasonable income but the maintenance payments do not reduce until she is earning more than average weekly earnings. A man might have become responsible for his new partner's children but that does not reduce his obligations. Non-custodial parents have to pay maintenance at the usual rate even when their children are staying with them in the holidays. Those who are rich will be paying sums far in excess of what is needed to support their children.

The percentage system makes child support look like a tax rather than a payment to support children. It might be better to strike a flat amount per week and make no one pay more than this. Poor men would pay much less (those on the dole currently pay $5) but men in work would know that when they had paid this amount they had met their obligations, and second jobs and overtime would allow them to get ahead. Or there might be three rates – for three lifestyle levels – since the Court believes that after divorce children should continue to live in the manner to which they have been accustomed. A fixed rate or three fixed rates might well bring more returns than the present percentage rates.

Resentments are bound to exist in a system of forced payments and it would be foolish to think they can be entirely removed. A British study of maintenance concludes that men are happier in paying maintenance when their ex-wife allows them to have good relations with their children. Resentment is high when they don't or can't see their children. Why should they pay maintenance when their children will be unaware that they are doing so? Our Family Court could have assisted in the collection of more money and the reduction of much resentment if it had obliged mothers to accept access by fathers that it had itself ordered.

Fathers who do not have access are still obliged to pay maintenance. All those in the family law industry are happy to live with this, which indicates how accustomed they have become to treating non-custodial fathers as non-people. It is understandable that fathers treated this way should object to paying maintenance. Here is the official explanation of why they must continue to pay, as provided by the Child Support Agency:

> To argue, as many do, that a non-custodial parent who does not see their child should be able to cease paying child support, overlooks the fact that child support is for the child, not the custodial parent. It is simply an assertion that the child should be punished by having their means of support cut off because of the behaviour of the custodial parent.

Notice first the exaggeration of "means of support cut off". A mother without other means of support receives the Parenting Pension (and all the concessions that accompany it), Family Tax Benefit A, Family Tax Benefit B and rent assistance. When she receives child support, the amount of Family Tax Benefit is reduced by fifty cents for every dollar received. That's what she would lose if, by denying access, she lost child maintenance.

Consider now the injustice of one institution of the state, the Family Court, giving a man an order to see his child, which it does not enforce, while another institution of the state, the Child Support Agency, assesses the man for child support, which it pursues relentlessly. A man who voices his justifiable resentment at this treatment is accused of wanting to punish his children. Consider further that a father may hope that in order to keep her maintenance his former wife may allow him to see his children. So a father wanting to see his children is accused of wanting to punish them.

How hard are these men to be driven in the best interests of the child? Their suicides give the answer. So that's in the best interests of their children!

The Child Support Agency will not reveal how many of its clients commit suicide, but there is a protocol for dealing with this regular occurrence. It was revealed after the ACT coroner examined the death of a 28-year-old man, Warren Gilbert, who gassed himself in a car clutching a letter of demand from the Child Support Agency. The general manager of the Agency said that suicides have a profound impact on their staff. In such cases the Agency goes back through their records to see if the client had given any indication that he was in distress over child support. Mr Gilbert had given no such indication.

The Family Court is a civil court where two sides present their case to the judge, who decides the dispute according to law. In other civil courts the cases are presented in a highly disciplined way, by what are called pleadings. These state the facts of the case as they are relevant to the law that is being invoked. In the Family Court pleadings were tried for a time and dropped. Parents representing themselves found them difficult and pleadings don't work well where the law is as vague as "the best interests of the child". Now proceedings begin with the parties presenting affidavits, sworn statements, usually of great length, which rehearse the virtues of the deponent and the shortcomings of the other parent. They are notoriously highly coloured if not mendacious documents.

You're reading these affidavits. She's not saying that about me, is she? I must defend myself. How can she say this, when she's done that? Then next minute it's this tit for tat nonsense. And it's so trivial. At the end of the day it's the lawyers making money out of it.

The speaker is Graham Sweetland, a tradesman, bronzed, well-knit and still handsome in middle age. His talk is lively and pithy, with occasional shifts into the legal language that he now knows so well. He is a leader of a men's group, but no one could be more critical of the fathers who fight for access and then fail to show up to collect their kids. *The kid is left standing at his mother's gate. They leave the poor little children without as much as a phone call.* He is annoyed to find that when fathers have custody of children they can be as nasty to the non-custodial mother as when it is the other way around. He is ashamed that he treated as friends men who have been found guilty of sexual abuse of their children. But his anger still flares over the men being driven to suicide as the Family Court leaves them *hopeless and helpless.*

He has the unlettered man's respect for education, which makes him more indignant at the behaviour of the educated men he has encountered at the bar and bench of the Family Court. *Lawyers! Respectable? Ned Kelly would shine all over these people. They're thieves with a licence.* Like many others, his contempt for the Family Court is founded on his discovery that though it is a court it is not interested in establishing the truth.

He spent $53,000 in a failed attempt to gain custody of his baby boy. Soon after he was born, his mother started acting strangely; it seems she had a complaint resembling post-natal depression. She believed the child was speaking to her at six weeks and giving her instructions about the best diet for him. She left the family home in Brisbane and went to live with her parents in Sydney. Husband and wife remained in touch. They'd watch the same TV programs – *Blue Heelers* and *Heartbeat* – and chat about them, while they were showing, on their mobile phones. Then after three months the wife announced that she had seen a counsellor who had told her she had married him for the wrong reasons. *I will only ever speak to you again if I have to.* She denied him access to the baby boy.

He felt that the boy was in danger in his mother's care and was told by his lawyer that he had a strong case for custody based on the mother's psychological condition. The mother did not want him near the boy. And so they entered the Family Court and complied with its mode of establishing who should care for a child: the two candidates did their best to blacken each other's reputation – or rather their lawyers did.

The lawyers not only encourage it; they are almost insistent upon it. They say: if you are not prepared to take my advice, why are you here?; if you haven't anything detrimental to say about your wife, then I am afraid she is probably going to get away with everything. What can I say? What can I say? OK. She's psychologically unstable – a thing you are reluctant to say about your loved one.

The loved one had plenty to say about him; accusations of drunkenness and violence. He had one conviction for assault. His defence was that he was trying to break up a fight. In a police interview his wife had given evidence to this effect, but now she was using this episode to stop him seeing his child.

She had also taken out an Apprehended Violence Order against her husband. These are very readily obtained. No violence has to have been committed; if the woman claims that she fears that her husband is likely to be violent, the magistrate will grant the Order. The man can contest it, but only with the greatest difficulty since it is hard to disprove an apprehension. The usual advice is to accept the order without admission. But in the Family Court the existence of an Order is taken as prima facie evidence of violence. Sweetland reports how he was conned into accepting an Order:

Mr Sweetland, by your own statement you are not harassing or stalking your ex-wife, nor do you have any intention of harassing and stalking her or anyone who resides with her. Is that correct?

Yes, your worship, that is correct.

So it would have absolutely no effect on you to have the AVO. Is that correct?

That is right, your worship.

So you will agree to the AVO?

Yes, I will.

But he hastens to add that he is opposed to domestic violence. Men who breach their AVOs should be punished. Nor is he opposed to AVOs, but they should not be used to label a man as violent when he has never been violent and remain on his record to his detriment.

Truth-telling is important to him. *If I'm lying to you, John, I am lying to myself.* When he read the affidavits submitted by his wife, he immediately spotted a clear inconsistency. His wife said that she was so distressed when she left Brisbane that she drove through the night and arrived in Sydney next morning. Her cousin said she was so distressed that she stayed with her in Brisbane for five days before she could travel south. *These are sworn affidavits. They can't both be true. One of them must be a lie.* He wanted his lawyer to make much of this to the magistrate. His lawyer was not interested. *I am quite sure he has read them.*

His lawyer asked him what access he was prepared to grant his wife if he gained custody.

I would give her excessive access. I would be happy for her to ring or even to come to my house at two or three o'clock in the morning if she was having any anxiety attacks about not seeing her baby.

The lawyer did not think his case would be advanced if this was reported to the Court. He is sad his wife did not learn of it.

While the custody was determined, the Court allowed him access to his boy. The magistrate explained that because of his wife's accusations, the access would have to be supervised. Since he had not seen his boy for some time, he agreed to this condition. The magistrate sensibly organised for his wife's parents to bring the boy to his home and supervise the contact.

Six weeks later on his next appearance in court, the magistrate granted him unsupervised access. The matter of his fitness as a parent was not argued out in court. His wife's allegations were not contradicted, just overlooked. He still does not know how he was rehabilitated – whether by his parents-in-law or a psychologist attached to the Court.

The personnel in the Family Court work within the static of false allegations, which their mode of operation encourages. They make their decisions according to their principles of what is best for the child and who knows how much notice they take of the allegations that fill the air. In this case they gave the father the standard deal – every second weekend and half the school holidays. He was poorly advised to fight for custody, which particularly for a young child the Court is reluctant to take from the mother.

However, ordinary citizens are not yet ready to be publicly defamed in a court of law. Graham Sweetland is bitter over the money he spent on lawyers and what happened to his reputation in the Court. *Guilty till proven innocent – in a democratic country. It's horrible, isn't it?* The magistrate probably doubted the wife's allegations from the beginning, but when he chose to ignore them he made no acknowledgement, let alone an apology, to the man. A decent citizen must simply be ready to accept that the Family Court will treat him for a time as a pariah.

I tell him I'm glad his spirit has not been broken by his experiences in court. It's not altogether true, he says.

I am a door-to-door salesman as well as a tradesman. It used to be; "G'day mate. I'm working in the area. I might not be better than the other bloke but I'm as good as him.

I've got good materials on the back of me truck. I can probably give you a better price than the other fellow. I haven't got as high overheads, TV ads and so forth." Now it's: "Mate, you want your roof painted or not? No? Righto, mate. See you." It has knocked the stuffing out of me. Somehow I can't seem to concentrate.

In his advocacy work Graham is buoyed by the certainty that the present Family Court regime is coming to an end. There will be no more lawyers and if allegations are made they will have to be proved. Indeed, the select committee that reported late in 2003 did recommend that custody cases be decided by a tribunal, not staffed with judges, and not operating in adversarial style.

Settling disputes between parents over the care of children in an adversarial way is madness. The best interests of the children are advanced if separated parents can co-operate, whereas the adversarial system promotes conflict between them. In acknowledgement of this, Justice Nicholson established an experiment in the inquisitorial method in the Sydney and Parramatta courts just before he retired, which is the best thing he ever did. In this style of justice the parents talk with the judge and the lawyers sit behind them, a reversal of the usual set-up. The same judge conducts all the hearings so that the parents feel they have someone in charge who knows their case. (Sweetland had ten Court sessions in thirteen months with a different judge almost every time; once two judges in the one day!) The judge directs the collection of evidence. Proceedings begin with the judge asking each parent what settlement they want and why it would be best for their children. So there is not the slanging match by affidavit – in fact, most cases are settled without the odious affidavits being necessary.

Because of its commitment to the best interests of the child, the Family Court has been zealous in uncovering child abuse and keeping abusers away from children. Can there be any quarrel with this policy? What would we not do to save a young girl from the nightmare of being sent alone to a father who uses her for his own sexual gratification?

The difficulty for this Court and for all others is that sexual abuse of young children is very hard to detect. There may not have been sexual penetration of the child. Without physical signs, the evidence is the child's testimony and though this is more reliable than was once thought, it can be vague on some details and disordered – and children are very suggestible. When experts are presented with the same evidence in an abuse case, they can give wildly differing conclusions.

An additional and peculiar uncertainty for the Family Court is that allegations of sexual abuse may be part of a campaign that one parent is waging against the other over custody of the children. The most common case is mothers accusing fathers of abuse; the next is fathers accusing the mother's new partner of abuse. The allegation might be an outright lie, more commonly it is no more than a suspicion that grows into a certainty in the hostility that accompanies divorce; it might, on the other hand, be well founded.

In 1988 the Family Court departed from the practice of all other courts in Australia that deal with sexual abuse. It established the new approach in its judgement in the case of M and M, which had its origins in a women's shelter in suburban Adelaide. In November 1986 a mother arrived at the shelter with her two children. This was not the first time that she had left her husband; there had been a number of break-ups and reconciliations. The boy aged ten was the offspring of a previous marriage; the girl was just short of her fifth birthday.

A fellow resident of the shelter, noticing that the girl was "bed-wetting and soiling", suggested to the mother that the girl might have been sexually abused. The mother immediately made an appointment with the Sexual Assault Referral Centre. The father was entitled to visit his daughter while she was at the shelter, but had not yet done so. If the girl had been abused, it was while the family was still together. At the trial the mother attempted to hide how and when the possibility of sexual abuse was first planted in her mind; she dated it to several weeks later, after the father had visited, and her own and the expert examinations of the child had begun. But the judge found that she had not concocted her story; she had genuinely come to believe that her husband had abused the child.

At the Sexual Assault Referral Centre the girl was examined by a social worker and the head doctor. To neither did she make any disclosures of abuse and the doctor found no genital abnormality. A month later the child visited her father. On her return the mother grilled her for information about abuse. The next day she took her to the Flinders Medical Centre where a physical examination revealed a somewhat enlarged vaginal entrance. The following day she returned to the Sexual Assault Referral Centre where the same social worker as before interviewed the girl and referred the mother to the Department of Child and Community Welfare. This option the mother seems not to have followed up. A week later the mother again took the girl to the Flinders Medical Centre. A physical examination again revealed that the entrance to the vagina was open and there was a slight reddening of the vulva, but no conclusive signs of abuse. The child was not distressed by the examination. A female constable from the Sexual Assault Unit questioned the child, but she made no disclosures.

The mother was now regularly quizzing the girl and keeping notes. She also taped conversations. From the tapes the judge was later able to determine that the mother was asking leading questions and putting pressure on the child to make revelations. The child said very little. The mother reported that during one of her conversations with the child, the girl made a drawing of her father's penis, which appeared to be erect.

The girl was kept in hospital for a few days. A week after her release she was interviewed again by the police constable, with her mother present. This interview was taped. The girl was questioned for a long time and made no statements that would implicate her father, but then under pressure and in response to leading questions she did for the first time make admissions to officialdom about oral and vaginal sex.

She was then taken regularly to a therapist, whose task was not to diagnose abuse but to help its victims overcome the trauma. The therapist was a Dominican nun with degrees in Arts and Psychology from Flinders University. To her the child made more admissions, and the therapist, more confident than anyone else, was sure the child had been abused and that the father was the perpetrator. The child was now very distressed at her visits with her father, which had become supervised visits once the allegation of sexual abuse had been made.

This was the evidence before the Family Court judge when the mother asked that the father no longer have access to his daughter. On the balance of probabilities – the normal test in a civil court – the judge ruled that he was not satisfied that the father had abused the child. He was impressed by the father, who denied any wrongdoing with his daughter. He appeared to be telling the truth and to be genuinely aggrieved at what he saw as false and unjust accusations. The wife, on the other hand, had given "conflicting and contradictory evidence" and the judge wondered why she had pursued the matter so relentlessly. The medical evidence gave no indication of abuse. The child's admissions emerged only under great pressure and in response to leading questions (particularly dangerous with young children – this girl was five). Nevertheless the judge still had a lingering doubt: perhaps the child had been abused. On this basis he ruled that the father could no longer see his daughter. He said, "No risk or possible risk should be taken which would endanger the welfare of the child."

The father appealed to the Full Family Court. Chief Justice Nicholson to his great credit – for this much can be forgiven – declared that the Court could not abandon some objective test; "lingering doubt" was not good enough. In nearly all cases, once an allegation of sexual abuse had been made, there would always be a lingering doubt. And how could a judge confidently determine that there would be no risk at all in the future? He continued:

> Some attempt must be made to quantify the risk before taking the grave step of refusing a parent access to a child. If this is not done there is a real danger that the mere raising of an allegation of sexual abuse will be sufficient to preclude the obtaining of an access order ... There must be a real or substantial risk of such abuse occurring as a matter of practical reality.

The two other judges would not follow their chief, and the father's appeal was dismissed. The father then appealed to the High Court, which without dissent dismissed the appeal. The court confirmed the approach of the trial judge, though for the future it defined the test as not lingering doubt but "unacceptable risk". So a new test had been introduced into the law. It was not, the High Court insisted, designed to judge the guilt or innocence of alleged perpetrators – which is not the concern of the Family Court – but rather to assess when it is safe in the interests of the child to grant access to someone accused of child abuse.

In endorsing this approach the High Court departed from English practice where a father found, on the balance of probabilities, not to have abused a child can continue to have access; and from the practice of the children's and youth courts of the Australian states, which decide abuse cases on the balance of probabilities. (Justice Nicholson referred in his dissent to English judgements.)

Professor Patrick Parkinson, the leading academic expert on Australian family law, has been quietly critical of the High Court's ruling in M and M. The Court, in laying down the "unacceptable risk" test, said that it was the normal business of the Family Court to assess risks. However, says Parkinson, normally the Court is assessing whether something that has happened might happen again. Now the Court was assessing whether something that might or might not have happened might happen again.

Courts normally deal with facts. Either the father had abused the child, or he had not. If the Court cannot or will not reach a determination on that point, then the Court, if it is serious about assessing risks, should move away from looking at discrete facts and assess whole situations. The Family Court has shown no interest in laying down procedures for doing this. Among the factors Parkinson suggests for consideration are the identity, personality and life history of the alleged abuser. As to identity, among the child's relatives, the biological father is the least likely male abuser; step-fathers and grandparents are much more likely offenders.

Professor Parkinson also reminded the judges that men kept from their children are human beings. The Court may say that they have not been condemned as abusers; they are just an unacceptable risk – but they might not be able to see the difference. It will be hard for a man who has not abused his child to think he has been treated justly. Further, while it is certainly in the best interests of the child to protect them from abuse, it is also in the best interests of the child to maintain contact with their father. Banning too many fathers is not good policy.

There is sexual abuse direct and abuse by suggestion. A mother who nurtures in her children the belief that their father has abused them is damaging them severely. The Family Court has not been so zealous in saving children from this abuse. Witness the case of *W and W*, decided in 2001, in which a father sought to have custody of his three daughters transferred from their mother to himself. The mother had adopted New Age spiritual beliefs and introduced her oldest girl, aged twelve, to them. According to the mother, the daughter became more proficient than she at communicating with spirits. The girl made elaborate accusations of sexual abuse: of herself by her father, paternal grandparents and an uncle, and of her sister by their father. The judge found the following:

The father was a reliable witness.
The mother and daughter were unreliable witnesses.
The paternal grandparents were reliable witnesses.

The husband did not sexually abuse the girls.

The grandparents and the uncle did not abuse the girls.

The children were not at risk of abuse from the husband or the grandparents.

These are unusually clear findings. The difficulty the judge faced was
that apart from her "complete lack of objectivity" on the abuse issue, the
mother was a good mother and the children were happy living with
her. He was prepared to leave the children with the mother if she would
now abandon her bizarre beliefs. He questioned her closely through her
lawyer. The lawyer did his best, but he could not hide the fact that the
mother still believed in her daughter's powers and hence that her husband was an abuser. So the judge placed the children with their father,
with the mother to have supervised access to them. He realised this
would be a wrench for the children and a heavy responsibility for the
father. He ordered counselling of father and children to help with this
transition.

The mother appealed and won in a two to one decision (with
Nicholson in the majority). The Full Court considered the judge had
acted precipitately, in particular by not ordering counselling for the
mother to see if she could be weaned away from her views. The trial
judge had obviously decided – it seems to me on good grounds – that the
mother was a lost cause and her views a danger to her children. So the
children were left with the mother and her court-appointed counsellor.

In a similar case Chantelle De Laine was left with her mother after the
mother had made unsubstantiated allegations of sexual abuse against
Chantelle's grandparents. Chantelle is her real name; she is now over
eighteen and wants the world to know how the Family Court damaged
her. She reports that her mother threatened to beat her if she did not
maintain accusations of abuse. She underwent therapy for abuse that had
not happened. By a happy chance she is now reunited with her father
whom the Court had kept from her. She sees her paternal grandparents

who were the alleged abusers. Her grandfather has not recovered from the ordeal. He was a prison warder and somehow word that he was an abuser of children reached the gaol. The other warders passed this information to the prisoners so that he would be appropriately dealt with. He had to be transferred and soon was invalided out. These accusations wreak tremendous havoc.

The Family Court, which regularly has to deal with cases of sexual abuse, has no expert arm of its own to examine them. It transfers all allegations, without any prior scrutiny, to the state child welfare departments. The staff in these departments face a huge workload, greatly increased by mandatory reporting, and they give priority to the cases where children are in immediate danger. Their test is "likely harm" not "unacceptable risk". They give a very low priority to family law allegations, knowing that a good deal of them are likely to be false, merely products of custody disputes. In many family law cases children are not in immediate danger: the father has already been put on supervised access or the accusation is of abuse of a step-daughter in a household he has now left. The result is that the Family Court waits a long time to receive reports on the matters it refers and they are frequently unhelpful when they do arrive. The other result is that the genuine cases coming from the Family Court get overlooked. Men have abused and even killed children because warnings have been dismissed as "just custody cases".

In 2002 the Family Law Council recommended that the Family Court be given its own expert body to deal with child abuse. The federal government has not as yet responded. I can understand its reluctance to be directly involved in such a difficult area. But the integrity of its own institution – the Family Court – is compromised by its reliance on the state bodies that examine allegations of abuse. I have not studied the workings of these closely, but I have learnt enough to have severe doubts about their competence. They can be both over-zealous and slack. The procedure to control abuse is now far from transparent and open. That is how it may have to be since children cannot be adequately protected by the normal methods of prosecution of abusers in a public trial and the test of innocent until proved guilty. But safeguards may be needed to ensure that these procedures are not leading to dreadful injustice. For instance, every report on abuse might come with a second arguing the case that no abuse has occurred. These departments at the moment report either that abuse is substantiated or not substantiated – not that it has not occurred.

A federal agency might set higher professional standards, so long of course as it was adequately funded. It would have less business if the judges in the Family Court took greater control over what was happening in their Court and subjected claims of abuse to some preliminary examination before passing them on for expert advice. Their policy of passing on all allegations has had a corrupting effect on the whole process.

The Court has in fact developed a method of improving its handling of abuse cases. This goes under the name of the Magellan Project, which began as an experiment in Melbourne on the initiative of Chief Justice Nicholson in 1997. One hundred cases were processed. The aim was to get more reliable results with fewer delays. The judge was more directive and the same judge was in charge of each case throughout the various hearings, together with the same group of counsellors. The Court worked closely with staff from the state child welfare department, who were promptly to provide reports on which the Court could act. The results were taken to be highly satisfactory – and they give an indication of how drawn-out these cases usually are. The time to resolve a case was reduced on average from seventeen months to nine; the number of court hearings reduced from five to three; and the decisions of the Court were more closely adhered to. Most importantly there were fewer distressed children. The parents were pleased to have the one judge dealing with their case. The report on this experiment said:

> in families who cannot solve their own problems and where chaos
> is ever present the moral authority and leadership of a judge
> seemed particularly important and effective.

This approach differs from the resort to counselling as the solution to all problems. It also demonstrated how much the Family Court would be transformed by an inquisitorial method of proceeding instead of the adversarial method of letting hostile parties batter each other.

The name Magellan was adopted for this project because according to the social workers who designed it that navigator had falsified the myth that the earth was flat. The myth that the designers hoped to expose was that allegations of abuse made in the Family Court were "more likely to be part of the family fight about divorce or separation than to be a real event". They identified the believers in this myth as judges, lawyers and the state protection services, that is, those closely involved in the business. The social work academics planned to show they were wrong. Professor Thea Brown and her colleagues looked at some 200 cases that had already been dealt with by the Court. They did not ask those involved in cases for their views and how they picked the false and doubtful cases from the well-founded; they looked at the files and classified types of abuse and abusers. As they proceeded, the "allegations" were treated as real events — and conclusions drawn from them. That is, what had to be proved was taken as proven! A key conclusion of this study was that only 9 per cent of allegations were false and that false accusations were no more prevalent in the Family Court than elsewhere. However, the 9 per cent figure was not reached from a study of the 200 cases. It comes from a smaller sub-study of a mere 30 cases. The researchers examined the files and decided on the 9 per cent figure without revealing on what criteria they operated.

A low figure on false allegations does not disprove the "myth". False allegations here mean those maliciously made. But in many cases where there is no real evidence of abuse, accusers have an honest belief that abuse is occurring. Only 22 per cent of the allegations in this study were substantiated by the child protection agency — which seems fairly close to the "myth" (real event unlikely). This study would not be worth our attention except that it was quoted by Chief Justice Nicholson and others to show that there was no problem about sexual abuse allegations in the Family Court or at least not one worth worrying about.

Professor Brown remained on the project, and she and her colleagues wrote the report at the conclusion of the Magellan experiment. By this time she had had close dealings with fathers who had been wrongly accused of abuse and she was no longer so complacent. In a 2003 article she wrote:

> It is clear that allegations are made against fathers more frequently than against any other family member and that the person making these allegations is most commonly the mother. Furthermore, many fathers are found not to be the perpetrators as alleged. This gives some support to the belief of fathers that their former partners pursue them with malicious allegations of child abuse.

We should respect the Professor for changing her mind, even though she has only re-discovered what everyone else involved in the family law already knew.

Whether their number was more or less than in other arenas ceased to be important; the men wrongfully accused were a very substantial human presence complaining to the Professor about the stigma that had been placed upon them. She was sufficiently moved to write, "It was clear that there was a need here to consider what, if anything, could be done."

The Family Court considers that it has no need to do anything about removing the stigma. It says its business is not to determine guilt or innocence on a criminal charge. That's for the criminal courts. That is, the judges will trash reputations, but not restore them. It is quite disingenuous for the judges to invoke the criminal courts because no charges would be brought there on the sort of evidence on which they and the child welfare agencies customarily rely. These men will not be prosecuted, so they cannot by this means clear their names.

The indifference of the judges to the plight of these men is astounding. Chief Justice Nicholson reported that quite commonly judges are approached by the fathers to clear their name, but their plight did not shift them from the standard answer: it's not our business. Their plight is as follows. As soon as the accusation of child abuse is made, it is assumed to be true. If the men retain access to their child, it is supervised access with the further proviso that they are not to take their children to the toilet or bathe them. They have to prove their innocence and to do this they may have to spend heavily to hire experts to counter adverse evidence from the child welfare agency (which can quite easily implicate an innocent man). The onus of proof has shifted to them. Their relationship with their child is difficult to continue under supervision and in any case will be severely damaged by the accusation. Even if they regain access to their child, it is rare for a definite judgement that they were not abusers to be made. Hence the demand to "clear their name".

How can the judges shut their minds to what is now happening in their court? Consider a "lingering doubt" judgement made at the same time as M and M and which went through the appeal process in tandem with that case:

> I am of the opinion that if after considering all the evidence I have some lingering doubt whether or not the husband has molested the child that it is my duty to err on the side of caution and safeguard the child even if this appears to be unjust to a husband who has not been proved to have molested the child. However access is not a right of a parent. It is to be granted when it is shown to be of value to the child and in its best interests.

It is chilling to find a judge brushing aside injustice. This better than any other statement takes us into the mental world of Family Court judges. They have persuaded themselves that the terrible deeds they perform have only the appearance of injustice. They know they must be labelling innocent men as child abusers and keeping them from their children, but they are not depriving the men of anything to which they are entitled because in Family-Law-Land no parent has a right to see a child.

Anyone who was not a Family Court judge would pause when their reasoning carried them to the defence of injustice. You would be desperate to find a way around this impasse and if it could not be avoided then to think how the evil might be lessened. To think, for example, how to deter people from making false allegations or how to restore the reputations of those falsely accused. Such thoughts do not appear to cross the judges' minds. They have supreme confidence in what they are doing; the confidence of their own virtue. They are pleased rather than distressed at what they are doing, for it shows how far they will go to defend children.

There is great danger in elevating one purpose as the only purpose to be pursued. This is the totalitarian impulse. We see its evils clearly in the extreme cases when the purpose was the racial purity of the German people or the defence of the proletarian revolution in Russia. But it should be remembered that the people who performed horrible deeds for those causes thought they were good causes. We all think the defence of children is a good cause, but we cannot pursue this as a purpose in whose name anything can be excused. If we were prepared to practise even more injustice than the Family Court inflicts, we could not save all children from risk of abuse. The greatest danger of sexual abuse to children after divorce comes from their mother's new partner, who moves in without any scrutiny.

Though the judges are not interested in deterring the making of false allegations, let us consider it. You imagine that when a mother accuses her husband of sexually abusing his own children a shocked silence falls upon the court. The judge in solemn tones warns the mother that she is on oath and that severe penalties exist for making false allegations. You imagine wrongly. The Family Court runs a poison-pen service. You can make these allegations from the comfort of your own home or from your lawyer's office. You fill in Form 4 (it is on the Family Court website). There is no statement on the form warning of penalties for making false allegations. You do not make these statements on oath as you do in the compiling of a normal affidavit. The only warning on the form is that your description of the sexual abuse should fit the official description of abuse. You do not even have to sign the form; it is enough that your lawyer sign it. This accusation at a distance must stop. Of course there is need for haste, for the allegations might be well founded, but when the Court is sitting these allegations should be made in open court with due warning and solemnity and when it is not sitting before a magistrate or justice of the peace.

It is proper that on the form there are no warnings of punishment for false allegations because there is none – or none that the judges care to invoke. It is almost unknown for judges in the Family Court to refer cases of perjury for prosecution. In many cases where allegations are found to be unsubstantiated the accuser did have an honest belief that abuse was occurring, but judges do find some allegations malicious. The makers of malicious allegations should be charged with perjury.

It is hard to know how the reputation of those wrongfully accused can be restored. Apologies might help. The best thing to be done is for the Court to abandon the "lingering doubt" test, rule on allegations on the balance of probabilities as other courts do (so giving the accused a verdict), and make decisions on access accordingly.

Let us now summarise the sort of court the Family Court has become when it hears abuse cases:

One citizen denounces another citizen for a horrific crime.
The accused is assumed to be guilty until the trial.
The onus of proof is on the accused.
At the trial the standard of proof is not beyond reasonable doubt; not on the balance of probabilities; but lingering doubts in the mind of the judge.
The punishment of the guilty is denial of access to their child.
There is seldom exoneration of the innocent.

This court of law has become a gross abuser of human rights.

JULIAN ASTON

On the TV news lawyers appear en route to court pushing trolleys loaded with files. Julian came to see me pushing a double-decker trolley packed tight with his own files. He has been through seven courts, mostly representing himself. He recites them to me: *Magistrates Court, Youth Court, Family Court, Full Family Court, High Court, Court of Summary Jurisdiction and Court of Family Matters in the Northern Territory.* This has been his life for over nine years. He has frequently been told to get out of the courts and get a life. His response is that he wants to see his daughter. And who can say what is the best way to preserve your mental health when you are accused of getting your four-year-old daughter to suck your cock? Julian's instinct has been to fight back.

Julian is dressed in a striped shirt with a dark vest. His black hair is held in a knot at the back of this head. He has an expressive, mobile face; his voice rises quickly. He is somewhat histrionic – but he does have a drama to tell. He has also the habits of a lawyer; everything is documented. After each climax in his story he lays his hand on the file – if he is not actually quoting from it – and says he can send me a copy. There are numerous tabs on the files and a master index. *You can't keep a court waiting. You have to be able to tell the judge where to find the document.*

I did ask for copies of the files. I have them beside me as I write. I can confirm what every judge, police officer and social worker involved in this case has discovered: Julian is a scrupulously honest witness.

His daughter, Natasha, was born of a very turbulent relationship. The mother and father were not regularly living together. The pregnancy was not planned. The mother already had two children from a previous relationship who lived with their father. The mother asked Julian if he wanted her to have an abortion. *I have always been very strongly pro-life. I said: "If you are prepared to carry the child to full term, I'll bring the child up if you don't want to. And the door would always be open to you. Always." She was quite happy with that. I have to be honest. She was very responsible. She gave up drinking; she gave up smoking.*

Before the birth the mother had walked out of their joint home in Adelaide. *She was impatient with me. I was not earning much and she was used to more.* She sought emergency housing from the state welfare department who said that she could only be helped if she had been abused. She declared that Julian had been violent to her and to satisfy the rules took out a restraining order against him.

I asked him if there was any basis to her claim of violence. *She herself used to flip out at times. Before she got pregnant, she didn't mind drinking and she used to smoke a lot too. Sixty a day. When she became intoxicated she became quite unpleasant. I remember quite a few stoushes with her. It is a difficult line for a guy to tread. You have to know whether to defend yourself or leave the scene. If you leave, you get followed. It's a very difficult situation. There were times when I pushed her.*

The couple remained in touch, the mother having withdrawn the violence order since Julian had been determined to contest it. He was present at the birth. He was called to the Maternity Hospital from a TAFE photography class and he has a photo of his daughter's birth, of which he is justly proud. There are four gloved hands lifting the baby from the womb, a circle of holy brightness in a swirl of dark. He held his daughter four minutes after the birth. *Her little eyes opened up. I know doctors say they can't see at that age, but she looked right up at me. I told her I'd always be there for her, but unfortunately I've been made a liar ... But enough of that.*

They entered the Family Court because they could not agree on how much access the father should have to the child. The mother wanted access to be supervised; she alleged that Julian was violent, that he was careless about the medication that controlled his epilepsy, and that he was an inexperienced parent. They were sent off to counselling by the judge. The counsellor saw the mother first. Soon the counsellor came out of the room and told Julian that counselling was finished. The mother had told the counsellor that Julian was a paedophile who had sexually abused her eight-year-old daughter from the previous relationship. This is known as allegation creep: the allegations get more serious as the case proceeds. The judge did ask the mother why she had not mentioned this grave matter in her first affidavit and got a very unconvincing answer. So now there was a supplementary affidavit. *I remember I was sitting in the parklands when I read the affidavit. I was in absolute tears. I was in absolute shock.*

The judge now had to determine whether a man accused of being a paedophile could have access to his daughter. On the basis of the new allegation, the mother was requesting that he have no access at all. Julian picks out the judgement of his first case and reads from it:

> The mother has alleged sustained and frequent attacks on her by the father. I have heard both of them give evidence. I accept the father as a witness who was truthful on this topic even to the extent of giving evidence prejudicial to himself. The mother's evidence on this topic, as on other topics, I find to be exaggerated, improvised and smacking of recent invention.
>
> The father has denied the mother's accusations with respect to paedophilia. I found him to be a convincing witness, admitting some matters to his detriment and giving the appearance of endeavouring to answer honestly. The mother on the other hand was not a credible witness. She improvised, exaggerated, gave conflicting evidence and as before some of her evidence smacked of recent invention.
>
> The evidence of Doctor Black and the father satisfied me that there is no unacceptable risk of the father not controlling his epilepsy. I find the mother's allegations to be another example of her exaggeration and willingness to clutch at any straw to thwart access.

The Family Court judge was quite sure that Natasha was safe with Julian but nevertheless he ordered only supervised access, not to protect the child, but to protect Julian. He was afraid that the mother would renew her allegations and he wanted Julian to have the protection of an independent witness. Julian had to pay for the professional person who supervised him. I was incensed at this on his behalf but among his other oppressions he took this as routine. *I wanted to see my girl. The mother was not going to pay. If she'd had to pay I would never have seen her.*

Julian saw his daughter (under supervision) only a few times because the mother broke an undertaking given to the Court and took herself off to the Northern Territory. Julian used a private detective to track her down. (These professionals suffered only short-term loss when fault was removed from divorce; they now find parents who are secreting children.) The Court issued an order for her to return to South Australia, but the mother ignored it. Mother and child and the mother's new partner stayed in the Territory, which meant that Julian could no longer see his girl regularly. He had to travel to the Territory and see her there or undertake the expense of bringing her back to Adelaide. Even this spasmodic access was regularly cut off or suspended or changed into supervised access by the Family Court because the mother did indeed renew her allegations against Julian. She accused him of horrendous sexual crimes against his own daughter.

The details had been elicited from the girl by leading questions from her mother in conversations which the mother taped and which every expert who heard them regarded as totally unreliable. The mother spoke of the abuse to everyone, to officialdom, to her friends and even strangers. She gave graphic physical details so that people were sickened by her accounts. She talked loudly about these matters in front of children and Natasha herself. By the time she was six, Natasha's conversation included details of what her father had done to her. Six times the mother made allegations that led to Natasha being examined by psychologists and social welfare departments of the Territory and South Australia. On another occasion after the girl had a playground accident Julian was accused of physical abuse, but the enquiry that followed quickly segued into another examination of sexual abuse.

All these enquiries decided that abuse had not occurred and that the girl was being coaxed into making the allegations. At the fifth enquiry the head medical officer of the child protection unit in Adelaide declared that

Natasha had been so sexualised by her mother and the previous enquiries that anything she now said would be worthless as evidence of abuse. But there was still another enquiry to come.

The findings of the judge in the first Family Court trial had no influence on this lengthy process. Neither the Court nor the welfare departments were ready to dismiss these allegations as coming from a totally unreliable witness, which would have saved Natasha another examination and Julian further pain and disruption to contact with his daughter. *She just keeps making the allegation. She's made it. It has gone to trial. The judge has found that it is not so. So she goes to the same court and makes it again. Instead of the Court saying that we've already judged that and found it to be rubbish, if you keep making these allegations we'll hit you with perjury, instead they say: let's go through the whole process again.*

Though no court had found him guilty, Julian was worried about what was on his file in the child welfare departments. When these departments receive allegations about child abuse, they are not obliged to inform the accused of what has been alleged against them or the results of their enquiries. The only way to obtain the details is through subpoena or Freedom of Information. Julian badgered the South Australian child welfare department about the first allegations made against him – concerning the mother's daughter from an earlier relationship. *So what's this "unsubstantiated paedophile"? That's basically saying that I am a paedophile but you haven't got the evidence yet. That's bloody outrageous. The requirement on me was to establish my innocence. I've done that, but you still won't let me be innocent.* He wanted a report that cleared his name, but he never got it. He spoke directly with the social worker who had actually investigated the allegations: *The Department had decided to support the mother and she* [the social worker] *had been ordered to destroy all hard-copy and electronic records of the outcome of her investigation.* These were the records that showed that nothing had been found to support the mother's allegations. This social worker subsequently resigned from the department.

When he took out a subpoena in the Family Court to get records from the Northern Territory child welfare department, the department there claimed it could not comply because the Territory's welfare legislation prohibited the disclosure of such information even to a court. So began Julian's ascent to the top of the legal tree. He challenged the Territory in the Family Court. The judge referred the case to the Full Family Court where Julian won. The Territory then appealed to the High Court. The case was becoming a *cause célèbre*. The Commonwealth and two states intervened. Julian lost. Meanwhile he had acquired the documents in question after his victory in the Family Court. After a five-year struggle he did get the department to reverse a judgement it had made on him. A police sergeant had reported that Natasha appeared to be coached, but that her allegations sounded convincing. On this flimsy basis and without further enquiry, abuse was found to be "substantiated", which is not what the sergeant had intended.

The mother's response to the constant rejection of her claims or any questioning of their legitimacy was to get another lawyer – she went through twenty-three – and to carry her complaints to government departments and welfare and charitable bodies. She used the allegations of abuse to claim special treatment in housing. She was regularly shifting house. She moved to Darwin to be close to a therapist who could help Natasha deal with her abuse. Abuse allegations having failed to destroy Julian utterly, she tried two new tacks. The police raided his house looking for child pornography – and found none. Over two years after legal proceedings in the Family Court had begun, she alleged that Julian was not the father of Natasha. He took a DNA test – and he was shown to be the father.

A welfare officer of the Salvation Army decided finally that Natasha was at risk not from her biological father but from her obsessional mother who was subjecting her to horrendous emotional abuse. As a result of her initiative Natasha was taken from her mother and put into foster care. There her socialisation began. She had become a little terror often uncontrollable by either her father or her mother. The father of course faced the added difficulty that the child believed he had abused her.

The removal of Natasha by the Territory welfare department occurred midway through another long hearing of the whole affair, now seven years old, in the Family Court in Adelaide. After all the allegations and uncertainty, Julian had asked the Court to grant him unsupervised access to his daughter. The mother was ordered by the Court to bring Natasha to Adelaide so she could be assessed by a child psychologist. The mother defied the order. Julian asked the judge to have her arrested. The judge refused. So the case proceeded in the absence of the mother (who had caused all the havoc) and without an up-to-date assessment of her daughter. The assessment was not to relate so much to the child abuse, but to the child's relationships with her parents. The psychologist knew from previous involvement in the case that Natasha now did not want to see her father. Julian called many friends who had supervised him on access to witness that there was a bond between him and his daughter, but the judge was not convinced. She was persuaded that there was a bond with her mother. Julian in his ingenuous way had told the Court that when he was having trouble with the girl she did enjoy talking on the phone to her mother and her partner, whom she now called Dad.

The assessment of Julian by this judge was the same as that made in the first full hearing seven years before. He was found again to be an honest witness and that there was no danger of his abusing Natasha to whom he was devoted, despite the trouble the devotion had caused him. The only fault the judge could find was that he sometimes raised his voice. But the judge thought that Natasha needed a rest from turmoil. Julian was to be denied access to her. The judge spared him one thing. She did not take up the psychologist's suggestion that he be given Family Court counselling for his grief.

It is anger that is in his voice as he completes his story. He is almost yelling at me. *I have never been charged. Every effort to investigate me has reached the conclusion that there is no evidence. Every trial judgement has reached the conclusion that I am an honest witness; that the evidence against me is made up; that Natasha is safe with me. But it makes no difference at all. There is no mechanism in the Family Court to get her tried for perjury. So she keeps on doing it.*

A new person took charge of Natasha's case in the Territory. Before her twelve-month foster placement was up, she re-assigned Natasha to her mother. She was completely dismissive of Julian's claims to see his daughter: "Julian has often described the Family Court proceedings as destroying his life; why does he persist?"

The mother took Natasha to Queensland. Julian has not seen her since. He knows her address, but he sees the point in not troubling her further. Like many dads kept from their children he buys her presents and agonises over whether it is better to send them and risk the mother destroying them or to keep them in the hope that the child later seeks him out. Then they will be evidence of his devotion.

You might think the judge acted wisely in keeping Julian away from his daughter given how matters stood. It is easy sometimes to agree with the judges when they ask what can be done with a determined vindictive parent who has the care of a young child. It might be worth trying what a more robust court could achieve. It would warn the mother that there would be severe consequences if she revived her allegations instead of making the father protect himself against them. It would certainly insist that she obey its order to return to Adelaide so that the child could have regular contact with her father. Above all it would refuse to countenance the re-opening of the same allegation.

The abuse of Natasha was before the Family Court in one form or other for almost six years. Other cases last longer. The judges watch while a parent continues to make allegations, so that the examination of abuse is a perpetual part of a child's life. Sometimes the cases have come to an end not when the judges intervene, but when the children grow up and call a halt.

In such cases, the Family Court, though committed to the best interests of the child, is itself a child abuser.

In his regular public utterances Chief Justice Nicholson spoke of what he saw as an oddity in Australian political culture – that failed litigants from the Family Court took their grievances to politicians. He complained that some of the politicians made the mistake of listening sympathetically, which encouraged these failed litigants to believe that their grievances were justified. Politicians, it appeared, were responsible for breeding opposition to the Court.

I suppose a man in charge of a court whose reputation is in free fall can be expected to be purblind about its causes – unless he is prepared to take some responsibility for the disaster, which Nicholson was never prepared to do.

The belief that his opponents consisted of failed litigants was the beginning of his blindness. These men formed only a small part of the fathers' protest movement. Many more were successful litigants who had the misfortune to hold access orders which his court would not enforce. Or they had failed to become litigants for lack of funds. Or they had been advised not to become litigants because they had no chance of seeing their children more frequently than every second weekend. Or they had been forced to become litigants to answer unfounded allegations against themselves. The fathers who joined the protest movement against the Court were often supported by their mothers, sisters and new partners. As the protesters formed into an array of permanent lobby groups, Nicholson did not give them any more respect. He had good grounds for objecting to some extreme groups, but he allowed them to colour his response to the wider movement. In a considered statement, opening the second annual conference of the Family Court in 1996, he characterised the supporters of so-called fathers' rights as "dysfunctional persons" with whom there was little opportunity for rational discourse.

Of course it is perfectly proper for citizens dissatisfied with the legal system to voice their complaints to their elected representatives. Nicholson was the one acting improperly, for there has never been an Australian judge less respectful of the separation of powers, which is meant to keep judges administering the laws and out of the arena that frames them. Nicholson campaigned openly against proposals to change the *Family Law Act*. Senator Brownhill (National Party), who was chiefly responsible for the setting up of the 1992 select committee into the Act, reported that Nicholson had written to him warning him off on the ground that politicians did not understand family law. Before the 2003 parliamentary committee had published its recommendations, Nicholson was publicly speaking against what he feared they would be. Nicholson's preference was that parliament not discuss grievances at all because this only raised expectations. Fathers thought the law had already changed, or changed more than it really had, and returned to the Court and re-opened their case. Nicholson saw this as harassing of their ex-wives. Some of it may have been, but Nicholson did not allow himself to think that a man shut off from his children might be renewing his efforts to see them.

Men had many grievances against the Court, but they made the proposal for joint custody their rallying cry. They charged the Court with being biased against fathers because it usually awarded custody to mothers. The Court's response was that if one parent had to be chosen to create a stable home for the child, then the Court was only following the bias of the society in choosing the mother over the father. Despite all the changes in gender relations over the last thirty years, generally it is still mothers who are more directly involved in the care of children. The Court could demonstrate that it was not inflexible on this issue because in the cases it decided custody was more often awarded to the father than in those which were settled by consent without a court hearing – the figures for 2000/2001 are 78 per cent to the mother in consent agreements; 69 per cent to the mother in trials.

This is a fair defence (so long as the premise of having to choose one parent is accepted). The burden of this essay has not been that the Court has been necessarily wrong to choose the mother as the custodian. It is very hard to argue against the mother as the best primary carer of a baby and a very young child. But having given the mother custody, the Court allows her to do what she likes. She can shut out the father, change the kids' names, make false allegations, defy the Court – all more or less with impunity.

The men arguing for change have opted for joint custody because it most clearly signals what is wrong with their experience in divorce. They become marginal to their children's lives. If they can still see their children it is usually only every second weekend, which does not allow them to live normally with their children; they are forced into the role of courting or entertaining them. The scholarly literature now supports their complaints in arguing that fathers can only remain effective parents if they can help, guide and discipline children in their everyday lives. Whether joint custody is necessary to achieve this remains the question.

It is a tribute to our representative system that parliamentarians have been responsive to fathers' complaints. This issue reached them not through the usual channels – the quality press, think tanks, Radio National – but by what they heard in their electoral offices. There has been bipartisan interest in the issue, but members of the Liberal and National parties have been more responsive. The fathers who have suffered most are poor and live in the outer suburbs and in the regions, now not Labor territory. Labor is also more aligned with women's lobby groups, and to support demands made by men looks like a retrograde move and maybe threatening to women. Women's groups have been properly concerned to protect women from violence in divorce, a case that is now well accepted. In principle the bulk of these advocates should have no objection to children having effective fathers, but there is an instinctual reluctance in some quarters to concede the point. Concerns about violence can be a cover for opposition to any change. Those who worry about violent men frequently give the impression that the majority of men are violent or that violence plays a large part in most marriage break-ups. In fact around 12 per cent of separating women nominate violence to them or their children as the reason for the break-up – a confronting figure but one which in no sense represents a majority.

The fathers and their organisations have been more successful in getting enquiries held than in getting the law changed. Unless someone with sufficient authority commands the issue and sees clearly what has to be done, change will be only incremental. Only twice since the foundation of the Court has there been a minister who has been ready to work for a substantial change. The first was Peter Duncan, a junior minister in the Keating Labor government who came to Canberra after a distinguished career in South Australian politics. He had been a reforming attorney-general in Don Dunstan's Labor government. In 1995 he made a great effort to change the law and failed. The second reformer is Liberal Prime Minister John Howard. It is too early to say whether he will succeed.

Labor has one interest in the *Family Law Act* not shared by its opponents: it was responsible for its creation. Duncan saw himself as the heir to Lionel Murphy, the reforming attorney-general in the Whitlam Labor government, who had been responsible for the Act. He planned to restore the Court to something like what Murphy had intended. He was scathing about the Court's elaborate procedures and self-importance, the staging of long and expensive trials instead of giving quick and cheap settlements. To fix this Duncan put more stress on mediation and provided more funds to support it. He saw nothing in the original Act to warrant the Family Court giving such full control over children to the custodial parent. This was the issue being pressed by the fathers' groups. He dropped the terms "custody" and "access" and replaced them with "resident" and "contact" to indicate that the parent with whom the child resided was not the custodian. (The old terms are still in common use and I have retained them elsewhere for ease of understanding.) The parents were to be joint custodians in the sense that they were to make decisions jointly over such matters as the child's education, religious upbringing and choice of career. The non-resident parent was also to have regular access to the child. Whether Duncan intended that this would produce joint custody in the sense that children would spend equal time with both parents remains problematical.

To emphasise the full involvement of both parents in the child's life, Duncan proposed a new section for the *Family Law Act* labelled "Objects and Principles" to guide the Court in making its decisions. This drew on the principles and language of the UN Convention on the Rights of the Child that Australia had recently adopted.

> a) Children have the right to know and be cared for by both their parents, regardless of whether their parents are married, separated, have never married or have never lived together.
>
> b) Children have a right of contact, on a regular basis, with both their parents.
>
> c) Parents share duties and responsibilities concerning the care, welfare and development of their children.

The UN Convention also spoke of the rights of parents, but this was carefully excluded. Nevertheless this formula envisaged a very different regime from that which the Family Court had constructed.

Advocates for women were very active as this Bill passed through parliament, and showed that at this level they operated more effectively than the men's groups. A special umbrella group called the National Women's Justice Coalition was formed for this lobbying. Its concern was that if fathers were to be more involved in the lives of children, women and children would be in greater danger from violent men. They persuaded the Democrats in the Senate to sponsor an amendment that made the new Objects and Principles apply *except where they were contrary to a child's best interests*. This caveat was placed immediately before the Objects and Principles. With the help of the Liberal opposition (such are the dynamics of oppositional politics) this amendment was passed in the Senate and became law. How far the caveat would affect the interpretation of the Objects and Principles would be in the hands of the Court. Elsewhere in the Act there was still the provision that the best interests of the child must be the paramount consideration in all decisions regarding children.

The *Family Law Reform Act*, as it was called, came into operation in June 1996. Duncan was no longer in office; he had lost his seat in the March 1996 election, which saw the defeat of Paul Keating as prime minister and the installation of John Howard. Now out of politics, Duncan wrote a very frank article for the press on the prospects of the new Act. He thought the parliament had sent a clear message to the Court about joint parenting, but he was afraid that the Court would ignore it. The Court had a well-developed sense of its independence and Nicholson had equipped it with its own media/public relations department. If the Court did ignore the parliament, he urged the government to carry a case on appeal to the High Court to bring the Family Court into line.

In July of the following year Nicholson made his riposte to the parliament when the Full Family Court heard an appeal on a location case. The trial judge had allowed a mother who had care of two girls, aged nine and eleven, to move from Cairns in Queensland to Bendigo in Victoria and so remove them from their father who also lived in Cairns. The father had the right to see the girls every second weekend, but by consent with the mother it was often more frequently. That contact would now cease; he would see his girls only in the school holidays. The father appealed against this decision on the grounds that the judge had not been guided by the new Objects and Principles of the Reform Act, which stipulated that the children had the right to regular contact with both parents.

Nicholson in a long judgement rejected the appeal and found that despite parliament's deliberations and enactments the law in essence remained the same. The Court would decide matters according to the best interests of the child, which the Act still enjoined it to do. Though the new section was called Objects and Principles, though its prescriptions carried the moral force of *rights*, though they had the sanction of the UN, though they were no ordinary amendment to the law but part of the new Reform Act, they were simply matters to be taken into account; they were not to guide the Court in any particular direction. The Court would not be bound by any fixed or general rules; the particular circumstances of each case would determine the outcome. Nicholson held to this view though the new Liberal attorney-general had appeared personally in the case to tell the Court that the law had changed and they should not decide cases on the principles they had used previously. Nor was the Chief Justice moved by the father's lawyer presenting to him Duncan's speech in parliament which demonstrated the intent of the law.

So it was not the caveat inserted by the Democrats to the Objects and Principles that stymied change. Nicholson simply refused to take the Objects and Principles seriously.

Why was it in the best interests of the children in this case to be removed from Cairns to Bendigo? The mother after being separated for five years had received an offer of marriage from an old friend who lived in Bendigo. He was a businessman whose business kept him in Bendigo. The judge found the mother to be an unhappy person with feelings of anger and persecution (over the break-up of the marriage, it seems) but also described her as "warm, spontaneous and articulate". She was also "a parent of exceptional quality" and to her credit had declared that if the Court did not allow her to go to Bendigo she would remain with the children in Cairns. The father too had excellent relations with his girls, "a caring and capable parent" according to the judge. Rather than lose contact with his girls he was now claiming custody, but if the mother remained in Cairns he was happy for the present arrangements to continue.

The judge feared that if he did not let the mother go to Bendigo she would become depressed and hence less able to look after her children. So it was in the best interests of the children to be removed from their school, their friends, their father and their father's family and placed at the other end of the continent. Nicholson and his fellow appeal judges found this reasoning to be impeccable. Family Court judges, though they see plenty of evidence to the contrary, are the last upholders of the view that women are fragile creatures.

What else might the judge have done? Since he had officially committed himself to the necessity of the mother and her suitor being conjoined (for the benefit of the children), he might have suggested that she regularly fly to Bendigo or he to Cairns. Instead he made the children fly from Bendigo to Cairns in the holidays. He might have congratulated the mother on her devotion to her children and expressed his confidence that she would cope with the disappointment of not going to Bendigo – for after all it would be to the benefit of the girls to remain in regular contact with their father.

By the Reform Act, parliament had wanted the Court to ensure that both parents remained involved in the lives of their children. How much importance did the Court give to these girls maintaining close relations with their father? None at all.

This case attracted wide attention and oddly for a time it did become harder for custodial parents to get permission to move, though the Full Court had decided the Cairns/Bendigo case in favour of the mover. But matters then returned to normal with about two-thirds of applications to move being successful. Within two years of the Cairns/Bendigo decision – in 1999 – the High Court signalled to the Family Court that it could be even less restrictive on permission to move.

Some argue that the Court should not constrain the movement of custodial parents at all. In the Cairns/Bendigo case the Human Rights Commission appeared to defend the right of freedom of movement. This was to miss the point. Of course the woman was perfectly free to go to Bendigo; the question was should she take her children or should they be transferred into the care of their father. If both parents are to be involved with their children after divorce, restrictions on movement have to be accepted. Parents in intact families forego much more to keep the family together.

The Court did not altogether ignore the 1995 Reform Act. It became reluctant to deny a father contact with his children even when he was accused of being violent (which is of course not the same as his being violent). Until the case was resolved, which could take months, he was allowed supervised contact. If the allegation was upheld, he would then lose contact. Some fathers gained slightly longer periods of access than every other weekend, but the broad pattern of life after divorce remained the same. The children lived with their mother and visited their father.

The prospects of real change seemed better when in June 2003 Prime Minister John Howard indicated his support for – or his inclination towards – joint custody. He was worried at so many young boys growing up with no contact with their fathers and without any male role model. This had become a widespread concern; attacked on this front the Family Court seemed more vulnerable than when it was accused by men's groups of being hard on fathers. Howard transmitted the proposal for consideration to the House of Representatives standing committee on Family and Community Affairs, which was to report within six months. It was asked to consider whether on separation there should be a presumption that children spend equal time with each parent and on what grounds the presumption could be rebutted.

Chief Justice Nicholson was the leading opponent of this proposal. He spoke against it publicly, before the committee, and his Court made a strong written submission to the committee in opposition. He was not in touch with the prevailing mood. He defended the Court's record on the allocation of custody and criticised the joint custody plan as being developed by fathers who were not thinking of the best interests of their children. But the starting point of the enquiry had been that it was not in children's best interests that fathers be excluded! He was concerned, along with women's groups, that the plan would yoke women to violent men. But the joint custody was rebuttable! – it was to be the starting point of negotiations and it could be argued against. A violent man would be the first to be excluded from it. Nicholson's chief point was that the plan was "a one size suits all" solution. This overlooked both that the plan was rebuttable (and hence adjustable to varying degrees) and that the present system itself produced a standard settlement: kids with the mother, fathers with access every second weekend. When pressed on this by the committee, Nicholson replied that in his court every case was treated on its merits and an individual solution crafted. In his court, yes; but in the 95 per cent of cases that were settled outside it, routine ruled as lawyers, mediators and counsellors made an informed assessment of how the Court would treat a standard case. The chair of the committee had real difficulty in getting Nicholson to think not of the complex cases he saw in the Court with entrenched conflict and violence and abuse, but of the standard cases with ordinary people, where if joint custody was made the starting point something very different could be established. In its public hearings round the country the committee was hearing from ordinary fathers who were dissatisfied without ever having had a full-blown trial before Nicholson and his colleagues. Nicholson seemed scarcely aware of their existence. The "failed litigants syndrome" continued to blind him.

Nicholson was on firmer ground when he listed the practical difficulties of joint custody: parents living too far apart (kids can't have two schools); children preferring one home; a high degree of co-operation necessary between parents. Generally the discussion of the difficulties was clouded by how the subject had been introduced. The Prime Minister took joint custody to mean a 50/50 time sharing. When Yuri Joakimidis, the scholar of joint custody and national director of the Joint Parenting Association, heard that formulation, he feared it had been used to stymie change since it is so easy to find objections to it. His formulation is that a joint custody settlement should "maximise the time and involvement each parent is willing and able to contribute in raising their children". As to the time, he is happy to see a range of between 40 per cent and 60 per cent, which can be achieved in a variety of ways, not necessarily week and week about. Perhaps he should be even more flexible. Getting the time to be quality time is the key thing. Why always weekends? A dad spending two weeknights with his daughter could help with homework and go with her to her netball practice. For young children short visits of an hour every other day would be more beneficial than a block of time every other week.

Do the fathers really want more involvement? About a third lose all contact with their children. Custodial mothers complain that fathers regularly do not show up for their access visits and they are left to explain the absence to disappointed children. The Joakimidis formula allows for this – willing and able. Surveys here and in Britain indicate that fathers are looking for more involvement. If the atmosphere of the settlement were different and more options available, more fathers might find it easier and more satisfying to remain involved.

The opponents of joint custody point out that many men are not closely involved with children in intact families. Why then do they claim an interest after the divorce? The answer in some cases is that men after divorce re-assess their priorities and decide to cut back on work in order to have more time with their children. And of course more fathers in intact families are now involved with day-to-day care of children. One of the victories of the women's movement has been to show that this task is gender-neutral.

Those who list all the practical difficulties should recognise that joint custody is in part a symbolic claim; it is a protest against automatic marginalisation and exclusion. The claim could be conceded and the practical difficulties allowed to work themselves out. A man offered the chance of looking after his children every other week may decide that their home can be with their mother so long as he has a say in when he can see them – and it might be more than every other weekend. And if his circumstances change, the option would be there for him to increase his involvement.

Late in 2003 the standing committee reported its findings. It is not clear why it baulked at recommending that joint custody be made law. The committee itself seemed committed to the change; the bulk of the evidence it heard was in favour; the Prime Minister had given them the cue. It properly recognised that there are cases where joint custody is inappropriate, but it seems it was not ready to let the process of rebuttal take care of these. Although not prepared to recommend it as law, it remained sympathetic to joint custody and in appropriate cases it urged that it be encouraged. Judges in the Court were to consider equal time. Consider it! Had the committee not heard what happened to Duncan's reforms? This court will *consider* anything, but it will *decide* things according to its view of the best interests of the child. The Court made it abundantly clear to the committee that it was opposed to anything like equal time or to doing anything differently. The only way to control the Court is to instruct it where the best interests of children lie. The Court could be told, in Joakimidis's words, that the best interests of the child will be served by maximising the time and involvement each parent is willing and able to contribute in raising their children – unless the Court finds on good grounds that the parent is a danger to the child.

The government broadly accepted the committee's recommendations. So it too believes that change can be effected by getting the Court to *consider* new options. (The government's plans are discussed in more detail in the Afterword of this essay.)

The committee had not been asked explicitly to consider the processes of the Court, but it boldly recommended that a new family tribunal be established to make decisions about the custody of children. There would be a panel of three composing the tribunal; proceedings would not be adversarial; the panel in inquisitorial style would be in charge of collecting evidence; the rules of evidence would not apply; and lawyers would be excluded (unless the tribunal ruled otherwise). But the rulings of the tribunal could only be enforced by the Court (this was a constitutional requirement) and cases involving violence and abuse were to be referred to the Court. It was a messy and an expensive proposal with a whole new institutional layer being introduced into the system. The cabinet rejected it after quelling a strong backbench push in its favour. It did adopt the recommendation that a system of shop-front centres should operate across the nation where counselling and mediation would be offered in an effort to keep parents away from the Court.

The making of the recommendation for the family tribunal supports my earlier claim that the Family Court is a failing institution. Those who want change have decided that it must be bypassed or supplanted. However, just at the death knock, Nicholson showed he was prepared to contemplate radical change. In his last year as chief justice he ran the experiment in the inquisitorial method at the Sydney and Parramatta courts discussed earlier. The House committee was aware of his plans, which may have encouraged it to make its recommendation that the Family Court itself move to an inquisitorial method. If this recommendation is implemented (the government has indicated its support), the Court itself would become much more like the proposed tribunal – and more like what Lionel Murphy originally intended it to be.

It used to be thought that the Family Court had to operate in an adversarial way to conform with our judicial processes. But now it is accepted that it could act in inquisitorial style, whereby the judges gather the evidence and the usual rules of evidence need not apply. The one catch that would disappoint Graham Sweetland is that lawyers cannot be excluded, which may make it difficult to get the proposal accepted (lawyers are a powerful lobby group). But with judges directing litigants to supply what they need, lawyers would be less necessary. In any case most people can't afford them.

It would be important that all cases be heard in the inquisitorial way. Sometimes proponents of an inquisitorial method exclude the difficult cases involving violence and child abuse. These are exactly those which will benefit from a judge directing proceedings – as is evident from the Magellan Project – and in halting proceedings. Remember the case of Julian Aston.

Already 40 per cent of litigants are running their own cases and an inquisitorial court would encourage more people to approach it unrepresented. Paul Walton could have approached such a court with confidence, knowing that establishing his fitness to see his girls would not have to hinge on rival lawyers cross-examining rival medical experts. But an inquisitorial court will be too much like the present court if it does not determine to enforce its own orders. Without this – as in Walton's case – people will still be told to stay away from the Court because winning a case would not necessarily mean success.

THE FAULT OF NO-FAULT

No-fault divorce has not yet led to no-fault weddings. Marriage services are now very varied, but in some form the couple make a commitment to each other. Not yet are there services where the couples declare:

> I promise you nothing.
> I will leave when I like.

These would be the words if services followed the principles of the *Family Law Act*.

Marrying is a moral act. Couples have views of right and wrong behaviour in marriage, as does society at large where "cheating" on your partner, even in these liberated times, is still commonly regarded as a betrayal. Some couples come to divorce agreeing without rancour that their marriage has failed, but more have a sense that the other partner has broken a commitment or has not understood the obligations. They will of course usually have different notions of who had what failings.

When no-fault divorce was introduced, it was promoted as a way of ending marriages which both parties agreed were over. It would rescue them from the hypocrisy and perjury of having to prove fault. However, no-fault divorce has worked in a way not envisaged by its proponents. It allows one partner to surprise the other with the declaration that the marriage is over without having to give reasons or undertake any negotiations on how fault will be acknowledged. So a new sense of injury arises in a regime of no-fault from a partner being able unilaterally to abandon the commitment to the marriage. In marriages where there are children, over 80 per cent of divorces are initiated by one parent – the woman in two-thirds of the cases and the man in one-third.

The difficulty of managing no-fault divorce is that most of the parties involved strenuously believe in fault. When they have children, they are urged most earnestly to put aside their injured feelings and concentrate on what is best for the children. Why should they? A woman after being regularly battered has just left a violent man; a man has just discovered that his wife is leaving to join her secret lover – and they are meant to sit down calmly with their partner and work out what is best for the children. In no other area of life would we expect people to swallow down their pain and hurt. We are very conscious of the need for these feelings to be voiced and heard and understood. Everyone knows that the arguments over children after divorce are frequently a proxy for the unresolved argument between husband and wife, but we have abandoned one way of this being aired (a trial for fault) and have seen no necessity to replace it with anything else.

As we have already seen, the no-fault principle penetrates the whole family law system. Fault does not affect the award of custody, which is determined by the best interests of the child. Custodial parents who then behave badly will be left alone unless they are damaging the children. They will even be left alone if they are flouting a direct instruction of the Court. No-fault also operates in the property settlement after marriage so that the property is divided according to the contributions the parties have made to its acquisition and enhancement and according to their needs after divorce. Consider a typical case where the only substantial asset the couple has is their house. Women are properly regarded as having contributed substantially to its acquisition by being the homemaker, even if they have made little or no financial contribution, and their claim on the house will be increased if they are, as usually happens, to have the care of the children. But this is the settlement no matter what the circumstances of the marriage break-up.

You can test your commitment to the no-fault principle by examining the following two scenarios. Do you support the settlement that the Court imposes?

Scenario 1
Wife is at home, primary carer of three children. Husband has many affairs. Wife is constantly humiliated, but forgives him. When he is

drunk, he can be violent. Then after firm promises he has another affair. She files for divorce.

Settlement: Wife keeps the children and remains in the house; husband leaves. He sees the children every second weekend and pays child support, 32 per cent of his gross earnings.

Scenario 2

Wife is at home, primary carer of three children. She wants to do some outside work, which will also help with finances. Husband cares for the children three evenings a week so that she can work. She has an affair with a fellow worker. She files for divorce.

Settlement: Wife keeps the children and remains in the house, into which her lover moves; husband leaves. He sees the children every second weekend and pays child support, 32 per cent of his gross earnings.

If you agree with both settlements, you should consider a career in the Family Court. I have tried these scenarios on many people and haven't found anyone who agrees with the settlement in the second scenario. Some are outraged; some want more information; no one immediately gives support.

Many men have the experience outlined in scenario 2. The break-up might not involve a new lover; the wife may simply say she wants to start a new life – which will involve depriving her husband of home and children. Men who have these settlements imposed upon them stagger from the Court buildings feeling that they have been in a nightmare world where all the usual standards have been inverted. They are driven to unfashionable declarations of their moral worth: I am not a wife beater; I have been a good provider; I have been a faithful husband; I love my kids; I am a good worker for the community. They cannot believe that there is a place, an official institution, where all this counts for absolutely nothing; where they are treated exactly the same as the husband in scenario 1, who they would say deserves what he got. And all that Nicholson understood of these men was that they were failed litigants!

The results of my small survey are confirmed by a properly conducted poll into the question of whether fault should play a part in the settlement of a divorce. It was commissioned by the Centre for Independent Studies in Sydney. People were presented with the following:

> It has been suggested that serious misconduct in a marriage (for example, desertion, adultery, drunkenness or abuse) should be taken into account when the Family Court decides the settlement following a divorce. Do you agree?

Those agreeing or strongly agreeing amounted to 75 per cent. This was the view right across society; there was very little variation between men and women, old and young, married, divorced or single. It is an oddity, to say no more, that a key institution in our society operates on principles repudiated by the great majority of the people. When no-fault was introduced it was said to have popular support as evidenced in opinion polls, but the question put to the people was: if two people agree that their marriage is over ...

Barry Maley, a scholar at the Centre for Independent Studies, uses these results to support his argument that fault should be reintroduced, not to the ending of a marriage, but in the settlement that follows. He has to tread carefully because he cannot allow his scheme to damage children; nor does he want it to be seen as punishing a guilty party as the old divorce laws did. His formula is that the partner who breaks up a marriage unilaterally should pay compensation in some form to the other partner. He argues by analogy from the consequences of unilaterally breaking any other contract. So his response to scenario 2 above is to suggest settlements that included these provisions:

> The wife, keeping the children, to surrender to her former husband her property interest in the family home and to forgo any claim to residence in it.

The wife to agree to 50/50 residence of the children, or to offer her former husband primary care of the children.

The wife, keeping the children, to pay rent to the former husband if permitted to reside in the family home, or to accrue a debt for rent not paid.

I have some sympathy for his approach, but it would involve the Court examining marital behaviour. Proof would have to be established of adultery, cruelty, drunkenness and so on. I am not sure that public support for the change Maley wants would hold up when this implication sunk in. This surmise is supported by the evidence in David De Vaus's new book, *Diversity and Change in Australian Families*, which shows we are quite confused in our attitudes to marriage and its ending. Most people believe that marriage should be for life (78 per cent), that couples should enter marriage without even entertaining the possibility of divorce (87 per cent), that it is too easy to gain a divorce (70 per cent). But if things don't work out and the couple is unhappy, the great majority believe that the marriage should end.

Our problem is that we hesitate to endorse a public morality that will be enforced or have consequences. What is worse than bad behaviour is being "judgemental" about it. We condemn people of past ages for being hypocritical, that is for professing in public a morality that they did not practise in private. We are reverse hypocrites; we refuse to support in public the morality which privately we believe in. One consequence of this is that public institutions cannot act firmly against wrongdoing. We hesitate to remove drug dealers and beggars from the streets or expel troublesome students from government schools, or disruptive tenants from housing estates — meanwhile gated communities, patrolled shopping malls, security companies and private schools flourish, which reflect our real values that we are no longer willing to make public values.

Not so long ago it would have been inconceivable that a court would indulge a custodial parent behaving badly or openly defying an order of a court. The Family Court justifies its behaviour by having only one standard: the best interests of the child. Forty years ago people were not uninterested in the welfare of children. If the Family Court's view had been pressed on them, they would have replied that it is in no one's interest for a public body to endorse or excuse bad behaviour.

So the Family Court embodies the contradictions of our age. Its actions offend our sense of what is right, but we have not the confidence to set it right, to supply new instructions that will rescue it from the no-fault morass. I have sometimes been harsh on Family Court judges, but it is our law that has encouraged them to throw off normal standards when they step into their Court.

I cannot see the way by which the Court can be rescued. Until there is fundamental change, it will continue to give offence. The Family Court is a monstrosity, a court of law that cannot by its no-fault charter be a court of justice.

Meanwhile there are some changes that will improve it. These are the changes this essay has recommended:

When the Court has been deliberately and persistently defied, the paramount interest for the Court is upholding its own authority.

Parents have the right to see their children unless they are found likely to do them harm.

Parents holding access orders to see their children should not have to pay child support if access is refused.

People accused of sexual abuse of children should not be left in limbo; they should be judged guilty or innocent on the balance of probabilities.

Accusations of sexual abuse should be made in open court on oath.

People making knowingly false allegations should be charged with perjury.

The Court should have its own professional body to investigate accusations of child abuse.

Proceedings in the Court should be conducted on inquisitorial lines.

The *Family Law Act* should declare that the best interests of the child will be served by maximising the time and involvement each parent is willing and able to contribute in raising their children – unless the Court finds on good grounds that the parent is a danger to the child.

Of these the one with the most far-reaching consequences may be the last. Yuri Joakimidis, whose formulation this is, has a rule of thumb that it is the parent, woman or man, who thinks they will control the children who breaks up a marriage. When both parents know they cannot throw over their partner and keep the children to themselves, then the temptations of divorce will decrease. Divorce can be very damaging to children and it should not be entered into unadvisedly, lightly or wantonly. If the *Family Law Act* began to drive down our very high divorce rate, it would be protecting the best interests of children in a way that it has not so far done.

AFTERWORD: THE GOVERNMENT'S PLANS

In November 2004 the Commonwealth government indicated its plans for changes to family law. The plans were made in response to the recommendations of the House of Representatives committee that been asked to examine 50/50 joint custody (understood as a 50/50 time sharing between the parents). The committee did not recommend writing joint custody into the *Family Law Act*, though it wanted judges, mediators and counsellors to promote it in appropriate cases. It did endorse joint parental responsibility (understood as the general direction over the child's life). These recommendations the government has accepted. The government did not accept the committee's radical proposal for a new family tribunal to decide custody cases, but it did accept that the Court itself should move to an inquisitorial mode. The government accepted and extended the committee's recommendation for shop-front family centres as the entry point into the family law system. The government now plans sixty-five Family Relationship Centres across the nation. Here parents will get advice and be encouraged to draw up parenting plans which will define how they are to share their parenting in the future. Parents will be guided by counsellors and mediators. The first three hours of these services will be free. Only if negotiations here are not successful will parents proceed to legal action.

The government's plans were set out in a Discussion Paper, "A New Approach to the Family Law System", which called for submissions on the details. Over 400 submissions were received by the closing date of 14 January 2005. The government's final proposals are still awaited.

Counselling and mediation are not new. They have been part of the Family Court from the beginning, and more recently the government has supported community organisations like Relationships Australia which provide these services. The aim of the national network of family centres bearing the same name is to induce all separating parents to go here first rather than to a lawyer; to settle matters in a non-adversarial way; and to settle quickly before conflict becomes entrenched. I hope they work; they will represent a fundamental change to the system if they do.

The danger is that some parents might see the centres merely as an obligatory stopping point on the way to legal action. They may get legal advice beforehand on how to behave. The government's proposed inducement for parties to enter counselling and mediation in good faith is to give the Family Court the option of awarding costs against a parent who has avoided this stage or not taken it seriously. But, as this essay has shown, the Family Court is the opposite of firm in dealing with wrongdoers. Unless the Court changes its attitude, this provision will not be a deterrent.

The government has opened one way of evading the centres altogether. It has provided that in cases where there is violence or abuse, parents should go straight to the Court. A woman who is escaping a violent man is not to be made to enter into close negotiations with him over the children. This is very proper, but the system of Apprehended Violence Orders makes it very easy to allege violence against a non-violent man and to have a document to "prove" it. The government acknowledges the problem, but its solution is the same: the Court can award costs against a party making false allegations of violence or sexual abuse. Why will a Court that has taken almost no interest in punishing malicious allegations start taking them seriously now? The government is envisaging a more robust Court — which is what this essay has called for — but it has no plans to make it so.

At the Family Relationship Centres, parents are to be encouraged to think of sharing time equally with their children or to take that as the starting point of negotiations. But a parent who does not want this arrangement will move the dispute to the Family Court for a legal resolution. What the law provides and how the Court interprets the law will then be crucial. The government, following the committee's recommendation, is only asking the Court to *consider* shared parenting time. How much consideration the Court will give it may be gleaned from the speech of the new chief justice, Diana Bryant, at the National Family Law conference in September 2004. When she reviewed the House committee's recommendations, she said it had resolved against equal time and hence left the Court to decide the best interests of the child in each case. She didn't mention the recommendation that equal time be considered by the Court. It looks like it has already been considered and abandoned.

However, unlike her predecessor, she recognised that the difficult cases that go to trial should not provide the template for all the rest. In the ordinary cases she thought that settlements should recognise that "the role of fathers in the lives of their children is changing" (a very mild shift from Nicholson's position). However, she did not see it as the Court's responsibility to give a lead on this. She put the responsibility on the counsellors and mediators. But if they do not have any legal backing, how will they persuade reluctant parents to consider it? We can be sure that many parents will continue to see divorce as a way of keeping the children and keeping out the other parent. This returns us to the advantage of writing into law the rebuttable presumption of equal time. For the difficult cases this option would be readily rebutted, but it would be the starting point for the rest.

The government does envisage changing the Family Law Act to make joint parenting responsibility law and to give the Court the option of switching custody if one parent is denying access to the other. The first oddity of these proposals is that the Court can already act in this way. The second oddity is that these proposals are to be subject to the test of the best interests of the child. Hence the Court will not operate any differently than it has in the past because that test is already its guiding principle. This will mean that in most cases joint parenting responsibility will be stipulated and that the Court will use its power to switch custody only very rarely as a solution to long, complex cases.

The best interests of the child can be interpreted in many ways. As this essay has shown, it has been used by the Court to abandon the enforcement of contact orders;

deny even a presumptive right in a parent to see a child;

allow custodial parents to change their children's names without permission;

keep parents accused of child abuse from seeing their children though no offence has been proved against them.

If the government and the parliament want to change what the Court does, they have to take the interpretation of the "best interests of the child" out of the Court's hands. Take the switching of custody as the answer to the perennial problem of access being denied. The way to make this work is to tell the Court that where there is a deliberate and sustained breach of access orders, custody will be switched to the other parent *so long as that parent is adequate to the task.* Don't let the Court play with its purist view of best interests, which so often means leaving things as they are. We believe that the best interests of the child are not served by access being denied; we believe that the best interests of children generally will be served if the Court acts firmly against wrong-doers. The judges are lawyers; they will do what the law says. If they are intelligent and caring, they will choose carefully the cases on which they make a stand so that children are not damaged. Not many cases would have to be resolved in this way before custodial parents took an entirely different attitude to access than they do now. This is teaching the Court how to be robust.

Robustness will be thrust upon the judges if they become inquisitors, in charge of the collecting of evidence and directing the course of the trial. The government has committed itself to this change. In her speech to the annual conference the new chief justice spoke enthusiastically about the inquisitorial experiment that Nicholson instituted. The signs are good. But watch for opposition from the lawyers. This is a change that will have far-reaching consequences for the legal system generally.

SOURCES

I have relied on three books to guide me on the provisions and interpretation of the family law: Patrick Parkinson and Juliet Behrens, *Australian Family Law in Context: Commentary and Materials*, 3rd edn, Lawbook Co., Sydney, 2004; Anthony Dickey, *Family Law*, 4th edn, Lawbook Co., Sydney, 2002; and *Guidebook to Australian Family Law*, 8th edn, CCH Australia, Sydney, 1991. Reported cases from the Court are found in *Australian Family Law Cases*, CCH Australia, Sydney, 1976→ and are referred to below as FLC.

2–3   "Within months of the Court opening": *Sahari and Sahari* (1976) FLC 90-086.

3   "contempt ... will not be tolerated": *In the Marriage of M* (1978) FLC 90-495, at p. 77,570.

3–4   *G and G* (1981) FLC 91-042, at pp. 76,360; 76,363.

6   "Family Court judges expatiate": The views of judges were collected in Australian Law Reform Commission, *Contempt and Family Law*, discussion paper no. 24, Sydney, 1985, pp. 52–3; and *For the sake of the kids: complex contact cases and the Family Court*, 1995, pp. 88–9, 95–6.

6   "To my utter disgust and dismay": Submission No. 68 to the 1992 Joint Select Committee on Certain Aspects of the Operation and Interpretation of the *Family Law Act*, Table Office, Parliament House, Canberra.

6   "I am very slow to attach": *Contempt and Family Law*, p. 52, emphasis added.

9   "not from lack of power": Joint Select Committee on the *Family Law Act 1975*, *Report*, Australian Govt. Pub. Service, Canberra, 1980, p. 62.

9   "a unique result within contempt law": *Contempt and Family Law*, p. 11.

9   "the Chief Justice should issue a directive": *Report*, p. 195.

9–10   "a fairly widely held view": Family Law Council, *Child Contact Orders: Enforcement and Penalties*, Canberra, June 1998, pp. 16, 41, 66.

10   As I write, it has been reported that a mother has been briefly imprisoned by the Family Court for denying access, *Age*, 16 September 2004, p. 3.

10–11   Alastair Nicholson, "Family Law in the Looking Glass", Opening Address to NSW Young Lawyers Family Law Seminar, March 2001.

10–11   Nicholson appeared sometimes to abdicate responsibility for enforcement, *Sydney Morning Herald*, 21 October 1998; for his efforts at enhancement see Leonie Star, *Counsel of Perfection: The Family Court of Australia*, Oxford University Press, Melbourne, 1996, pp. 151-2, 210-11.

15   "rehearsed, wooden, brittle": Patrick Parkinson and Juliet Behrens, *Australian Family Law in Context*, p. 882.

18   *Brown v Pedersen* (1992) FLC 92-271, at pp. 79,010, 79,011.

18   "No relationship short of husband and wife": *K v B* (1994) FLC 92-478, at p. 80,970.

19   *Cooper v Cooper* (1977) FLC 90-234, at p. 76,250.

19   *Cotton and Cotton* (1983) FLC 91-330, at p. 78,252.

20   "As one respected judge put it": *Sampson and Sampson* (1977) FLC 90-253, at p. 76,358.

20–1   *Cooper v Cooper* (1977) FLC 90-234, at p. 76,254. In 1986 the Family Court in a rare decision ordered access to the father even though the child was opposed, but significantly had to rely on another NSW Supreme Court decision to do so: *Keaton and Keaton* (1986) FLC 91-45, at p. 75,435.

22   The paradox is formulated by Warren Farrell, *Father and Child Reunion*, Finch Publishing, Sydney, 2001, pp. 111–2.

22   "In their mediation work, the Court's counsellors": John Dewar and Stephen Parker, "The Impact of the new Part VII of the Family Law Act 1975", *Australian Journal of Family Law*, vol. 13, 1999, p. 111.

22   "how can we be biased": *The Times*, 10 November 2004.

23   "One judge ... opined": *Chapman and Palmer* (1978) FLC 90-510, at p. 77,676.

24   *Parkes and Parkes* (1982) FLC 91-231.

26   "not to be changed unilaterally": *Kelley and Kelley* (1981) FLC 91-002, at p. 76,075.

27   "a high proportion of divorced fathers": Jerry Silvey and Bob Birrell, "Financial outcomes for parents after separation", *People and Place*, vol. 12, no. 1, 2004, pp. 46–57

27–8   "Forcing people to leave their jobs": *Report*, p. 365.

29   "A British study of maintenance": Jonathon Bradshaw et al, *Absent Fathers?*, Routledge, London, 1999, p. 227.

29   "the official explanation": Jan Bowen, *Child Support: a practitioners' guide*, Law Book Co., Sydney, 1994, p. 85.

30   Warren Gilbert: *Canberra Times*, 19 November 2000.

38   "the judge still had a lingering doubt": *M and M* (1988) FLC 91-958, at p. 76,932.

38–9   "Nicholson to his great credit": *M and M* (1988) FLC 91-958, at p. 76,927.

39   "quietly critical": "Child Sexual Abuse Allegations in the Family Court", *Australian Journal of Family Law*, vol. 4, no. 1, March 1990; "Family Law and Parent – Child Contact: assessing the risk of sexual abuse", *Melbourne University Law Review*, vol. 23, 1999.

40   "the case of *W and W*, decided in 2001": Recent cases are available on the Family Court's website.

42   "In 2002 the Family Law Council recommended": *Family Law and Child Protection: Final Report*, Canberra 2002.

43   "The report on this experiment said": Thea Brown et al, *Resolving Family Violence to Children: The Evaluation of the Magellan Project*, Monash University, 2001, p. 94.

44   "more likely to be part of the family fight": Thea Brown et al, *Violence in Families: The Management of Child Abuse Allegations in Custody and Access Disputes before the Family Court of Australia*, Monash University, 1998, p. 89.

44–5   Alastair Nicholson, Keynote address to the 7th Australasian Conference on Child Abuse and Neglect, 19 October 1999; Submission (no. 751) of Family Court of Australia to Standing Committee on Family and Community Affairs Inquiry into Joint Custody, 16 August 2003, p. 37.

45   2003 article by Thea Brown: It is odd, given the myth-busting purpose of the Magellan Project, that this concession was not included in the official report on the project but in the author's own article, "Fathers and Child Abuse Allegations in the Context of Parental Separation and Divorce", *Family Court Review*, vol. 41, no. 3, July 2003, p. 378.

45   "It is clear that there was a need": Thea Brown, *Resolving Family Violence*, p. 81.

46   "I am of the opinion": *B and B* (1988) FLC 91-957, at p. 76, 922.

56   "Sometimes the cases have come to an end": Thea Brown, *Violence in Families*, p. 91.

57   Nicholson on oddity of the political culture: *Sydney Morning Herald*, 21 October 1998.

58   2000/2001 figures: *Every Picture Tells a Story: Inquiry into child custody arrangements in the event of family separation*, Report of the 2003 House Standing Committee on Family and Community Affairs, 29 December 2003, p. 22.

59–60 Violence nominated as reason for break-up: David De Vaus, *Diversity and Change in Australian Families*, Australian Institute of Family Studies, Melbourne, 2004, p. 222. In the category of abusive behaviour, physical violence to you and children rates at 9.6 per cent; emotional and/or verbal abuse 2.5 per cent; alcohol/drug abuse (not directed) 11.3 per cent.

62 Peter Duncan, *Age*, 17 October 1996.

62 Nicholson's comments rejecting the appeal: B and B: Family Law Reform Act 1995 (1997) FLC 92-755.

63 Judge's comments in Cairns/Bendigo case: B and B (1997) FLC 92-755, at p. 84,177.

64 Figures on permission to move: Patricia Easteal, Juliet Behrens, Lisa Young, "Relocation Decisions", *Australian Journal of Family Law*, vol. 14, no. 3, 2000, pp. 234–58; Parkinson, pp. 1011–2.

64–5 On effect of Reform Act: John Dewar and Stephen Parker, "The Impact of the New Part VII", *Australian Journal of Family Law*, vol. 13, no. 2, 1999, pp. 96–116.

66 Yuri Joakimidis, *Back to the best interests of the child; towards a rebuttable presumption of joint residence*, Joint Parenting Association, 2nd edn, 2003, p. 162.

71 Initiation of divorce figures: Australian Bureau of Statistics, *Marriages and Divorces* 2001, p. 103.

74–5 Barry Maley, *Divorce Law and the Future of Marriage*, Centre for Independent Studies, Sydney, 2003, pp. 87–8.

75 *Diversity and Change in Australian Families*, Australian Institute of Family Studies, Melbourne, 2004, p. 231

77 "When both parents know they cannot throw over": There is some evidence of this already from those parts of the United States where joint physical custody has been adopted. See Maley, pp. 65–6.

Paul Kelly

No Australian prime minister within my experience has been "pervasively" or "systematically mendacious" (Billy McMahon excepted). Raimond Gaita makes this claim against John Howard, but, as far as I know, he has never established the evidence to sustain his proposition. It is an extraordinary claim – that Howard's mendacity is integral to his conduct of the office. I believe that Gaita misunderstands Howard, misunderstands how prime ministers operate and misunderstands politics in Australia.

There is no doubt, however, that he reflects and contributes to a view held either with world-weary cynicism or passionate intensity by many Australians and many influential Australians. In the process he assists neither Howard's critics (still clueless about how to beat him) nor the wider debate about politics and ethics.

No competent PM will lie on a regular or capricious basis. This is not just because it is unnecessary and politically dangerous to do so, but because a political system built on falsehood will risk internal collapse as well as external hostility. The first problem with Gaita's essay is the faulty empirical analysis upon which his argument rests. The purpose of my article (*The Weekend Australian*, 28–29 August 2004) that Gaita criticises was not to excuse Howard but to try to put his lies into historical context.

My argument was that lies – and big lies – have been a reality of prime ministerial power and that Howard has no unique status on this measure compared with his predecessors; that lies and deception, from war to the economy, tend to be driven by policy failures or political failures (that is, the lies are symptoms of a deeper problem); and that truth in politics is important but not an absolute.

Policy results are usually more important in moral terms than assessments of whether or not a government has been mendacious. Let me elaborate – how should one judge the morality of a government that never lied but whose economic failures were directly responsible for a recession that left a million people unemployed or whose national security ineptitude resulted in the death and injury of a number of its citizens? I am sure the Australian people would form a harsh moral judgement about such a government, and treat with derision any moral self-justification it offered based upon its honesty and its avoidance of "pervasive mendacity".

It is a neat polemic that Howard lied on both children overboard and Iraq's weapons of mass destruction. But these are quite different situations and each needs to be assessed on merit. At this point we don't know whether the Prime Minister lied about the children overboard, but the circumstantial evidence against him is strong. The evidence on Iraq is that Howard believed what he said about the weapons of mass destruction; that is, he did not use as a justification for war claims that he knew were wrong or that he suspected were wrong. (Of course, further disclosures might alter such assessments.) In both cases the public has been misled.

I believe the "breach of trust" campaign, despite its elements of validity and the intensity with which it is waged, is weak overall and is really the search for an organising moral principle to condemn and de-legitimise the Howard prime ministership across the board. Seen in this way, its defect is obvious – it is asked to carry too much. The claim of "pervasive mendacity" is an exaggeration and the idea that the immorality it represents should be the sufficient ground for the people to vote Howard out is a judgement devoid of any balance. Howard's election counter-attack, based on the notion of trust, exposed the weakness of Gaita's position. Trust is a more complex concept than his essay encompasses, a point he recognises yet resists.

In particular, trust is tied irrevocably to outcomes – whether in economic, social or military policies. Gaita's position – if I understand him correctly – is that the Iraq war is morally wrong and, as a result, even if much good resulted from the war, that fact could never redeem its immorality. He argues that because the intervention is wrong, the coalition can take no credit for the good consequences but must accept responsibility for the bad consequences. My own view is that the morality of public policy cannot be so divorced from its consequences. A smooth transition to democracy in Iraq would have helped the moral legitimacy of George Bush's position just as the deterioration over the past eighteen months has undermined it.

I say this neither to exonerate Howard nor to justify any lies or distortions. Gaita says he expects me to explain what could have justified Howard's lies, but I don't seek or need to justify these at all. My view that Gaita has misread the Howard government and has a flawed analysis of morality in politics does not mean that one is defending Howard's lies.

The problem for Gaita is that, having depicted Howard as a moral reprobate, he has also to explain his re-election by an increased majority. The trap for the moralists is that they might blame the people. The alternative is to offer rationalisations for the vote. But they avoid the obvious – the fact that their depiction of Howard as a moral reprobate and their insistence that the election be seen in these terms was a mistake. History will show that this interpretation of Howard by his influential critics has helped him, and that it has undermined the formulation of an effective, realistic and broad-based line of attack against Howard on the issues that are important to the people and in a language they find acceptable.

Gaita argues that war should only be a last resort and I agree. This is the reason I declined to support the war on strategic grounds. Iraq was a war of choice and the absence of any weapons of mass destruction suggests that the choice was an unnecessary one. It is a strategic folly to think that every genocidal dictator should be eliminated by regime change.

However, I remain unconvinced by many of the moral arguments. There was, for me, something disconcerting about the worldwide demonstrations two years ago when the middle classes of the rich democracies marched for the moral cause of keeping the Iraqi people enslaved under a tyrant, with many demonstrators dishonestly claiming to speak on behalf of the Iraqis.

I also have trouble with the moral tests that Gaita applies – notably his claim that no person should ever be treated as a means to an end and that evil (presumably killing) cannot be justified for a good end. These are excellent in the abstract, but what are the consequences of their literal application in the war against Islamic extremism? Given that Osama bin Laden has formally declared that the murder of any American anywhere on earth is the "individual duty for every Muslim who can do it in any country in which it is possible to do it" and that his terrorist organisation seeks a weapons of mass destruction capability to use against the American people, it seems to me that Gaita has taken a moral stance doomed to be unsustainable in this conflict. The war against terrorism remains in its early phase and much of the debate revolves around the subject of Bush's incompetence. However, the grave risk for the liberal left lies in its embrace of a moral principle that is untenable – given that democratic leaders have a political and moral obligation to safeguard their peoples.

It seems to me that the Australian people bring their sense of realism and scepticism to these issues and this is typified by their response to the Iraq war.

The people knew we went to war because of the US alliance, a point that Howard fudged. From the start they had no appetite for this war and, if Australia had to be involved, they preferred a very limited role (something that Howard ensured). They knew when Howard ordered the military deployment but pretended no decision had been taken on war, that, in effect, he was lying. They knew that Saddam Hussein, with or without his weapons of mass destruction, was no threat to us, but they accepted the world was likely to be a better place without him. They knew the exercise was a calculated risk in strategic terms and that its moral justification would depend upon creating a better Iraq. They know that Iraq has turned out a lot worse than Howard suspected and they know that Bush has severely miscalculated. I think, overall, the people are suspicious of the extreme claims advanced by both Bush and his moralistic critics and that these are healthy responses.

Finally, and in a wider sense, I fear the morality that Gaita wants to impose upon political leaders is simplistic in the extreme. At times he seems in denial about the compact of democratic governance. Governments have a responsibility to govern and that often requires inflicting hurt upon people (higher taxes, lower benefits) that would be unacceptable in the moral relations between two individuals. Political leaders have multiple responsibilities to their party, their supporters, the public and the national interest, and such responsibilities are often in conflict. Their job is to construct policies, to sell them and to persuade. Leaders select the advice they want; they operate as advocates; they are agents of partisanship.

Yet Gaita argues that "mendacity" captures many forms of untruthfulness and "more insidious forms of dishonesty than lying does". He tells us that a mendacious person "might lie, he might evade, he might intentionally muddy the waters and he might do any of these things sincerely ..." and, as I understand him, he wants to apply these standards to politics. Yet in politics the waters are muddied to begin with – political judgements, usually, are imprecise and uncertain and often made in the face of uncertainty as to the facts and the truth.

Let's take a famous example. In 1996 Howard won an election after saying he would never have a GST. Using Gaita's test Howard should have said something like this: "As you know, I have long supported an indirect tax. My pledge means that I won't introduce the tax this term but, depending upon circumstances, I may try to introduce the tax in a later term." This would not have been a responsible political statement. It would have been a disservice to Howard, to his party and to the community. (A similar argument can be mounted with respect to Keating's income tax commitment at the 1993 election.) I see no other way to interpret Gaita's argument than that this is exactly what he thinks Howard should have said. Yet this denies the essential craft of politics and its partisan nature.

I accept the sincerity of Gaita's position. But the more I read him the less I am convinced that under his rules our politics would be enhanced either in practical results or moral quality.

Paul Kelly

Paul Bongiorno

Two weeks before the 2004 federal election, the Sydney *Sun-Herald* carried the front-page headline "My Husband Does Not Lie". Mrs Janette Howard was quoted accusing those attacking her husband's veracity of attempting to manipulate attitudes for political purposes. In that she was no doubt right.

That she took the highly unusual step, for her, of entering the public debate in the heat of the election campaign is ample testimony to the fear in the Liberal camp that these attacks had the potential to undermine the government's re-election prospects. The fact that they did not has left many in Australia, to quote Raimond Gaita, "shocked, disheartened and bewildered".

One of the more disheartened, Robert Manne, has come to the sad conclusion that most Australians don't value issues of truthfulness and humanity as highly as he. But I am not sure this view is right. Ever the optimist, I have not yet joined that army of the disillusioned, "unsure about what to make of their country".

John Howard was emphatically re-elected although, in the first week of the election campaign, a Liberal Party official in Queensland swore in an affidavit that the Prime Minister's chief protector in the children overboard Senate inquiry, George Brandis, said of him, "He's a lying rodent" and "We've got to go off and cover his arse again on this." Brandis in a counter-sworn statement denied saying this. Almost simultaneously Mike Scrafton was swearing to the inquiry that he had told Mr Howard, before the 2001 election, that no one in Defence believed children had been thrown overboard. There was no evidence to support the claim and the navy video was inconclusive. For Howard's opponents, his mendacity is an open and shut case. They would not vote for him with a gun at their head.

But I believe many others, although critical of him on this matter, did vote for him. Labor's Bob McMullan on *Meet the Press* in early December 2004 pondered why it was that thousands who voted Labor in the *Tampa* election deserted the party for the Coalition this time. If these people were motivated by disgust over the lies and cruelty last time, why weren't they confirmed in their views when more evidence was in? I believe the answer has two parts. First, the case against Howard is not as clear-cut as his more strident antagonists claim. And secondly, while philosophers can and must argue abstractly and in a discursive way, voters have to make a concrete choice.

John Howard accepts that he misled the Australian people when he claimed that children were thrown overboard and stated, "I certainly don't want people of that type in Australia." He also accepts, somewhat more grudgingly, that he misled the Australian people over weapons of mass destruction in Iraq. But in both cases he pleads that he himself was misled. He was not being mendacious or lying because he did not set out to deceive.

Maybe only a Royal Commission into truthfulness in government as it applies to both cases could get somewhat closer to the facts. But I don't think so. Such commissions are inevitably tainted by politics and as such merely confirm prejudices already alive in the community. The Marks Royal Commission set up by the Richard Court Liberal government in Western Australia more than ten years ago is a good case in point. It found that the former premier and Labor high flyer Carmen Lawrence lied on three counts over the Penny Easton affair. It recommended charges of perjury be laid. Three were, only to be thrown out by a jury. The key point was that the jury believed Dr Lawrence's failure of memory. She was not on balance, as far as they were concerned, deliberately lying. That doesn't stop Dr Lawrence's federal opponents branding her a liar, or at the very least untrustworthy.

The Senate inquiry, after hearing from Mike Scrafton, former Defence liaison officer in then minister Reith's office before the 2001 election, found his evidence to be credible. The non-government majority also found it credible that he contemporaneously told a couple of naval officers what he had said to John Howard in phone conversations. The problem is that only John Howard and Mike Scrafton directly participated in the phone conversations in question. Many who abhor the government's asylum seeker policy see it as reason enough to think the worst of the Prime Minister. But if Howard was so deceitful, why did he release the inconclusive video two days out from the election? Could it be precisely because it was inconclusive, as Scrafton says he told the Prime Minister? Maybe a jury, if not a Royal Commission, would also give Mr Howard the benefit of the doubt. It's not unreasonable to suggest many voters, even though they were uneasy with the policy in 2001, gave him the benefit of the doubt in 2004. In other words, their vote wasn't a cynical discarding of the moral underpinnings of a genuine democracy.

I found Professor Gaita's discussion of the morality of war interesting and challenging. He gives short shrift to the "war on terror" but accepts that "for the defence of community, politicians will always do evil if they judge it to be necessary. Most people know that and most people expect it of them under pain of irresponsibility." But no such latitude is extended to Bush, Blair or Howard over the invasion of Iraq and, more broadly, the war on terror. Indeed it seems to me Gaita's view is that calling it a war is at best a metaphor, but one used with no legal or moral justification.

While the "Christian triumvirate", as they are called in the essay, linked terror to Saddam Hussein as a further justification for the invasion of Iraq, there is a body of evidence, convincingly compiled in Bob Woodward's book, *Plan Of Attack*, which shows that as far as the US President was concerned, September 11 was only an excuse to finish off the Iraqi dictator. But what if Australia's own participation in the war had a broader justification than that? What if it arose from a judgement that our national interest and survival lay with staying close to America?

If we accept that the security of the nation demands that prime ministers can't tell all of the people all of the truth all of the time, maybe we can excuse Howard's dissembling over the pre-positioning of our troops in the Middle East. Remember, the government insisted no commitment to an attack had been made, only that the option was being actively pursued. But then the argument becomes one of the relevance of Iraq to Australia's security. For those who see no relevance, then the Prime Minister has no justification for his lack of candour. But for those who see al-Qaeda and its fellow travellers as introducing a different paradigm, then Mr Howard's stance is a defensible one. Especially his linking of Australia's need more than ever to cleave to the United States in such a new and uncertain environment. Surely we have to accept the existence of a transnational phenomenon dedicated to the destruction of the Western culture of which we are a part. This is not paranoid, right-wing delusional thinking. The argument is over the best way of handling this threat. Is Howard's way making things better or worse? This I submit throws a different light on the whole issue of the government's morality and the electorate's endorsement of it.

The Prime Minister, of course, gave as the main reason for joining the invasion the disarming of Saddam Hussein. An all-party parliamentary committee found the government was less than frank about the way it presented the intelligence it was receiving from our own agencies. But John Howard wasn't alone in believing the Iraqi regime possessed such weapons. The Labor opposition at the time, as well as opponents of the invasion in Europe, expressed similar beliefs. The argument was over timing and process.

The daily bloodshed in Iraq is bleak testament to America's failure of planning and its lack of understanding of what was before it. Many would say it is a damning indictment of the foolishness of the policy. The President's own father, George Bush Snr, warned some years earlier that such an invasion could see America bogged down in that country for at least seven years. Yet while many will argue the Bush/Howard way is making matters worse, what now is the alternative? Howard understood instinctively that a majority of Australian voters would not countenance a weakening of commitment to the American alliance as an acceptable answer.

When John Howard asked whom voters would best trust with their security, he was not doing this in a vacuum. Rather than resorting to bravado to mask his record of untruthfulness, the Prime Minister was appealing to a reality. The reality was his record of bolstering the American alliance. The alternative prime minister, Mark Latham, was presenting a record of undermining it. He had foolishly attacked the American President personally as dangerous and incompetent, indeed as the most incompetent president in living memory.

Like Professor Gaita, I grew up in central Victoria in the '50s. He was one class below me at Saint Patrick's College, Ballarat. During World War II, Ballarat hosted American GIs for rest and recreation. The citizens of my home town welcomed the Yanks as saviours. Though I was born at the end of the war, my parents and their friends still had stories of the young Americans in their dashing uniforms. Australians in my experience have never been reluctant to acknowledge this debt. It is, I believe, part of our national psyche. Mark Latham's clumsy promise to withdraw Australian troops – what was left of them – by Christmas was a misreading of this deeper political reality. It fed the perception that he would put the alliance at risk. Many may have been ill at ease with John Howard's closeness to George W. Bush, but they would prefer it to the alternative on offer, scarcely concealed antagonism.

Raimond Gaita says, "To trust someone you must do more than believe him. You must believe in him. You must believe that he is essentially truthful." This is certainly true of personal relationships. But there is a significant difference in the relationship between voters and candidates for leadership. Their choice is limited only to what is on offer. It could come down to whom do you trust more or whom do you distrust less. Howard's question to voters on whom they trusted with interest rates and the economy had the credibility buttress of eight and a half years of record-low interest rates and a growing economy. The alternative, Mark Latham, had been less than a year in the leadership and he made only a belated attempt to calm fears on his economic credentials. Howard's pitch even survived the fact that when he was treasurer in the Fraser Liberal government, interest rates were higher than under the previous Whitlam Labor government and he'd left a $10 billion black hole in the budget. It survived because the Prime Minister was able to truthfully point to his government's record.

Breach of Trust is a discussion a genuine democracy with accountable government needs to have. The most powerful insight of the essay serves as a wake-up call for all of us. "Once one acknowledges that morality does not serve our interests but is their judge, then one will be free of the illusion that one can always creatively adapt it to serve our interests. Then one can acknowledge that morality and the world are not always suited to one another. To do this is to do no more than to acknowledge tragedy." The fact of the matter is no one side of politics or one particular leader has all the virtue or all the vice.

Paul Bongiorno

Mungo MacCallum

In a moment of cynicism I once defined a politician as "a man or woman who honestly and sincerely believes that the worst thing that could happen to the country is for him or her to be voted out of office".

This is, of course, an unfair and exaggerated generalisation: self-belief does not always translate into megalomania. But it is a rare politician who does not have the conviction, held honestly and sincerely, that his or her own interest happily coincides with the public good: *l'état, c'est moi.* Indeed, in some cases it becomes almost a matter of divine right; President Nixon is reported to have said something to the effect that any act performed by himself as president could not, by definition, be deemed a crime.

Faced with this kind of certainty, any normal person's attempt to apply normal standards of morality is, inevitably, doomed to failure. It is not simply a matter of ends and means. Rather, retention of power by this peerless individual is so overwhelmingly desirable that it justifies any amount of skulduggery in the process – whatever it takes, in the words of Labor's arch-manipulator Graham Richardson. The underlying premise is that the removal of the said individual would in itself constitute a great wrong – a sin against the public weal. The avoidance of this evil is in itself the overriding moral imperative.

It is an idea that John Howard has sold to the electorate with considerable success. Last year I was interviewed on ABC radio about my book *Run, Johnny, Run* which is highly critical of Howard's regime. A number of listeners rang the studio to voice their disapproval and in the process to accuse me of treason. *L'état, c'est Johnny.*

But while Howard's actions make it clear that he is at one with Richardson that the acquisition and retention of power transcends all ethical considerations, he still understands the need to pay lip-service to conventional morality. Thus he sets up a code of conduct for his ministers, even if he has not actually enforced it for many years. He constructs a firewall of unaccountable advisers between himself and the public service so that he can plausibly deny knowledge of any information which could cast doubt on his own integrity.

His statements are hedged around with lawyer's fine print, or even a highly idiosyncratic interpretation of language: thus the promise that there would "never, ever" be a GST should be understood to mean "not in this term of government" – although in fact it meant "not until I think I can get away with it". The fact that any reasonable person would take his words at face value is irrelevant; as with Humpty Dumpty, Howard's words mean what he wants them to mean, no more and no less. Mendacity is, then, not really possible.

Howard has tried to live down the ironic nickname Honest John to the extent that he now cherishes it as a compliment: John Howard is the man the voters can (and, it appears, do) trust. He may even believe this himself. If he does, then while one may accuse him of self-delusion, it becomes more problematic to say that he is actively immoral.

In the old days, in opposition, Howard espoused (or at least pretended to espouse) a truly ruthless standard of political morality. Here he is on telling the truth to parliament:

> Gough Whitlam had the guts to sack Rex Connor because he inadvertently misled parliament. He had the guts to sack Jim Cairns because he inadvertently misled parliament and his Prime Minister. We want to know if Paul Keating has the guts to sack Senator (Graham) Richardson because he misled the Senate. The supreme test of the courage and probity of the Prime Minister is whether he insists on ministers observing the basic requirements of a minister; that is, that they tell parliament the truth.

No ifs, no buts, and inadvertence is not a defence.

On that basis the present front bench would be very sparse indeed and Howard himself would be long gone. But of course, Howard's departure would be a far worse evil. The greater good supersedes the lesser. This, I fear, is the new political and ethical reality which Howard's critics (among whom I include Raimond Gaita) have failed to grasp.

In a famous exchange, the American writer F. Scott Fitzgerald remarked to his friend Ernest Hemingway: "The rich are different from us." "Yes," replied the down-to-earth Hemingway, "they have more money." But that was not what Fitzgerald meant.

Similarly, politicians are different from us. It's not that they are more (or less) moral; it's just that they are different.

Mungo MacCallum

Natasha Cica

Raimond Gaita does his own essay some disservice by calling it "abstract and discursive". However described, Breach of Trust is worth the mental exercise. First, because in it Gaita gently explodes some false dichotomies that have a peculiar and unhealthy grip on contemporary Australia. Shared pride against collective shame; commerce against integrity; security against decency; love of country against common humanity; ordinary "battlers" (who do real work, and understand nation-building, bone-cracking mateship) against spoilt "elites" (who don't, preferring divisive, effete chatter); patriots against un-Australians. Secondly, because the examples Gaita chooses to enliven his theory are provocative in our political context. His questions about terrorism and torture – laid like lines of salt on the weeping wounds of reconciliation, prolonged and cruel detention of asylum seekers, and the Iraq military intervention – revisit precisely the topics that the people most invested in those dichotomies wish would vanish forever. Breach of Trust reminds us that although today these subjects are largely swept under the carpet of mainstream Australian conversation, they are our nation's unfinished business, and this has practical as well as moral implications for all of us.

The prognosis? Gaita asserts that we "have every reason to think things will get worse", and "are suffering not just a decline in the standards of political behaviour but a serious illiteracy about the nature of politics". He means a kind of moral illiteracy. Standards of literacy on this front have no necessary connection with social status and levels of formal education – even in the humanities, even in moral philosophy. This revisits an old point about Germans schooled in the finest nuances of Goethe and Rilke nonetheless delivering the Final Solution. The converse also deserves mention: that the so-called "Righteous Gentiles" of Europe, non-Jews who risked their lives in World War II to save their Jewish neighbours from the Holocaust, had nothing much in common in terms of whether and what they'd studied, or adherence to formal creeds or political manifestos. According to an Israeli I once met who'd interviewed Righteous Gentiles to find what made them tick, one thing they did have in common was the capacity to think critically and question the given order of things. They also had healthy self-esteem. They also remembered moral guidance from their youth; not along "discipline and punish" lines, but in terms of remembering some particular adult who had somehow enhanced their understanding of the consequences and potential of their own behaviour.

It may be no coincidence, then, that Gaita illustrates his meaning of moral literacy with exemplars from his own childhood. Native-born Australians in country Victoria in the 1950s; his Yugoslav-born Romanian father, a gifted blacksmith with four years of primary schooling; and his father's closest friend, fellow immigrant and escapee from communism, Pantelimon Hora. In *Romulus, My Father*, Gaita gives a fuller account of what these people shared that was good, despite their differences:

> [My father and Hora] were not proud in any sense that implies arrogance, and certainly not in any sense that implies they wanted respect for reasons other than their serious attempt to live decently. I have never known anyone who lived so passionately, as did these two friends, the belief that nothing matters so much in life as to live it decently. Nor have I known anyone so resistant and contemptuous, throughout their lives, of the external signs of status and prestige. They recognised this in each other, and it formed the basis of their deep and lifelong friendship. But I know from their disappointments that they longed for a community of honourable men and women who humbly, but without humbug, know their own worth and the worth of others.
>
> Character – or *karacter* as they pronounced it, with the emphasis on the second syllable – was the central moral concept for my father and Hora. It stood for a settled disposition for which it was possible rightly to admire someone. The men and women in Baringhup and its surroundings in the '50s respected character even when, rarely, they had little of it themselves. Honesty, loyalty, courage, charity (taken as a preparedness to help others in need) and a capacity for hard work were the virtues most prized by the men and women I knew then.

Romulus, My Father provides a deeper sense of what drives Gaita's abiding attachment to the notion of common humanity, and his acute and clearly pained sense in *Breach of Trust* of the quality lacking in Australian political powerbrokers. The lack to which he points is one of due modesty as much as anything else. In that space, now, we have an oversupply of greedy tubthumpers and fraudsters of a range of political stripes, determinedly getting themselves ahead at any human cost. *Karacter*, of course, is not easily fooled by the spiv strata with their shiny costumes and fast numbers. It's focused on what people can and do deliver in the longer, harder, leaner haul. It says you know no one until you've shared a bag of salt. Unfortunately, *karacter* is not a core criterion for pre-selection or promotion in public life. It should be.

Australia is in the throes of a bad democratic stumble. Not only because the dominant political culture rejects some of the virtues that prevailed in the 1950s among both immigrants and the native-born, but also because it revisits some of the vices of the time, and that also takes us backwards in terms of morality. As Gaita tells it in *Romulus, My Father*:

> Those were the days before multiculturalism – immigrants were tolerated, but seldom accorded the respect they deserved. It occurred to few of the men and women of central Victoria that the foreigners in their midst might live their lives and judge their surroundings in the light of standards which were equal and sometimes superior to theirs. That is why it never seriously occurred to them to call my father by his name, Romulus. They called him Jack ... For proud men such as [my father and Hora] were, the condescension of their neighbours must have rankled.

Multiculturalism did subsequently land in Australia, both as political fashion and as genuinely lived at a range of human coalfaces. But this lump of condescension and rankling described by Gaita never quite melted – it never quite does, not anywhere – and has regained bitter currency in the post-Keating era. A direct line can be drawn between the failure of the otherwise good men and woman of Baringhup to really "see" Romulus Gaita, and the contemporary Australian-of-many-generations who asks Romulus's son, decades later when we should all know better, "Why don't you and your fucking Jewish wife leave the country?"

Despite his family background, it's far less likely Raimond Gaita, citizen of Australia, would have been on the receiving end of that kind of message if he'd kept his mouth shut about politics, morality and humanity. If instead, perhaps, he'd spent his working life in Australia selling European import leather lounges, or running a funky Balkan-Asian fusion restaurant, in some zone of affluence with cosmopolitan pretensions. Which points to the truth that cultural assimilation is just as much about the ideas and emotions you serve up at dinnertime as the presence of garlic and bok choy. It's as much about what moves you, the angle at which you collide with what you find, as it is about bloodline and birthplace. Consider how Gaita writes in Breach of Trust of his father's friend Hora:

> Occasionally, however, his tone and demeanour expressed something different ... Love of the goodness that he had read about, or seen in the people in his village in Romania, one of them his mother. Then tears sometimes came to his eyes. The way he was moved moved me and I learnt from it ... He spoke spontaneously of what mattered to him more than anything ... he believed, as Socrates did, that nothing was more important, "in youth or old age, than to discuss how one should live".

One long evening in 2001 I was sitting at my desk in Parliament House in Canberra, where I was working for a federal member of parliament. The phone rang. It had been running hot all night, while a political melodrama unfolded minute by minute. This was Tampa time. Far away, hundreds of displaced people sat on the exposed deck of that big red ship awaiting their fate at the hands of our elected representatives. The caller was an elderly Australian. She was a Holocaust survivor from Vienna, now living in Ivanhoe, a well-heeled part of Melbourne. She wanted to talk about how the plight of those men, women and children was giving her nightmares, again, about what she'd lived through over half a century before. She wept. She wanted me to understand why what Australia was doing was so very wrong. I listened, then left the office. "What's wrong with you?" asked a now-prominent Australian politician I met soon afterwards, seeing my face. Too clearly moved, I suppose, by the way my caller was moved, I recounted the conversation. "Serves her right for living in Ivanhoe," came the snappy answer. I learnt a lot from that brief exchange. I'm fairly sure the politician in question has forgotten it.

Gaita's moral economy has obvious roots in the material poverty of native-born Australians of the 1930s Depression era (some lessons of which have lingered longer in "backward" places like the country Victoria of Gaita's childhood, and the semi-urban Tasmania of my own), and in the dislocation of refugees pushed from Europe by World War II. These cohorts are clumped together in my head as the Fowler's Vacola generations, people whose survival has depended on knowing how to grow, sew, build, craft, conserve, save up and do without. With some lingering exceptions, their role as prime actors in Australian public life is effectively over. Too soon we'll reach a stage of our national life when they disappear from our private lives as well. Which leaves us with their successors, homegrown urban and suburban Boomers, as the most overwhelming gravitational force shaping Australia's public and private morality. The prospect does not thrill me. Only because their collective *grundnorm* is material comfort, generally attained far more easily from a start-up position than in generations before and since. And getting too much, too easily, has to get in the way of *karacter*. That's not a hymn in praise of masochism, poverty or juice-less puritanism. It's just a reminder that economic imperatives can cut both ways. And that economic trends can and do shift, like the fashions in politics and morality accompanying them.

This also means that *karacter* will again have its time in the sun, even though change along those lines anytime soon seems unlikely, and even if the pendulum first swings to darker places. Here it's worth recalling another defining quality of those Righteous Gentiles – a belief that things would improve, one day, and that the choices of each individual can make some difference to that. And that even if they don't, life is a miracle. Even where, as Gaita puts it in his essay, politicians do the terrible wrong of "intentionally, or just through carelessness, erod[ing] the conditions under which citizens, often through a love of country, form and sustain a love of the world despite the suffering and the evil in it".

Time to revisit the Old World, perhaps, for some more home truths and perspective. Consider these lyrics by Nenad Jankovic, from the soundtrack of last year's movie *Zivot je Cudo*. It's a love story set against the ultra-nationalist Bosnian wars of the 1990s, by Sarajevo-born, Paris-based, former Yugoslav director Emir Kusturica:

> Life is a candy
> With a red hot chilli pepper
> Filling inside.
> Life! Are you ready?
> You'll be a butterfly in
> The ultimate fight.
> ...

I remember that time
When life was a miracle.
As if Zidane played
For Liverpool.
Life is a business,
Risky and confused.
God gave you a deal
That you cannot refuse.
Life is Terrorism,
Globalism, Optimism.
Give peace a chance,
Give war romance!
...
But little did I know
Mr Preacher man
What real life could do
And shit could hit the fan.
Life is beyond peace and war,
Justice and crime.
Do you remember
That time?
When life was a miracle.

Call me aspirational, but that deserves an Australian coda:
Zidane pre-selected for Werriwa!

Natasha Cica

Alex Miller

I felt heartened and enormously stimulated by Raimond Gaita's words, as much
by the extraordinary eloquence and clarity of the argument – which was beautiful to read, and which left me with a sense of a great humanistic and poetic
sensibility behind the writing – as I was by the revolutionary nature of what I
took to be the main point: namely, that we are, as a culture and therefore as individuals, being asked for the first time whether we are willing to consent to the
use of torture, and therefore to become complicit in the practice of evil on our
behalf, and that to consent even to a discussion of the pros and cons of such a
proposition is already to accept an invitation to enter the arena of the damned.

Unless we are members of an extreme religious sect, we know ourselves to
be part of an evil world and that good, such as it is, is not exclusive either to our
own actions or those of our culture, but never before have we, as Gaita says, been
openly asked to consider whether or not we should be party to something that
we know to be evil. There are three possibilities: we say no, or we remain silent
– in which case complicit – or we say yes and damn ourselves outright. And no
doubt we qualify all these responses, even the firm no, and in doing so qualify
the nature of our response.

When my friend Max Blatt told me it was not being tortured that broke his
heart – he was tortured by Nazi experts for months and eventually thrown onto
the street and left for dead – but the eventual realisation that his torturers were
his brothers and that their roles may in other circumstances have been reversed,
I didn't question the validity of what he was saying. I still don't. I respect his
conclusion. I find it shocking, of course, but I believe it has been amply demonstrated that given the right conditions we are all capable of torturing our fellow
human beings. People didn't feel comfortable with Max's conclusion at the time.
Twenty years ago we all found it too shocking to imagine that Jews might themselves become the torturers, so Max was dismissed – as was usually the case with
nearly everything he said – but now it is common knowledge that the Israeli

forces torture prisoners – often they don't even bother with an elaborate denial of it any more.

What is shocking is that torture has at last come out into the open among us under its own name. The Chinese used to call it re-education, the Russians brainwashing, and in America it has had any number of elegant names – Australians, of course (I speak ironically), don't torture people, so we have no other name for it than torture. B. F. Skinner respectably imagined a landscape of human society beyond the, until then, sacred notions of individual freedom and dignity and condoned experiments in the name of psychology quite as extreme as torture. John Cowper Powys in his wonderful 1934 novel *Weymouth Sands* made vivisection, or live animal experimentation, the central evil in the world he created. We all know such things are torture for the victims, no matter what they are called by the people who justify their practice. And 3000 years ago Homer wrote a great book on the tragic futility of war and saw then that massacre and torture are commonplace in human societies. But what is it that has changed for us today that we are now calling torture by its real name and are no longer attempting to disguise it with some other, more seemingly respectable, word and are asking ourselves if after all it may be permissible among a civilised people?

Is it, as I think Raimond Gaita is saying, that our culture is on a slippery slope towards a condition of deep moral decay, even a kind of eventual spiritual demise, or is it that we have reached a point where it has become possible for us to acknowledge openly the awful truth about ourselves? I read Jacob Rosenberg's profoundly moving new book, *East of Time*, about the Lodz ghetto, in proof last week and went for a long walk afterwards feeling depressed. It had convinced me (once again) of evil. Which will sound naive, but I have always resisted accepting the idea of evil and have often let myself forget that it exists. I need to be reminded. And certainly I have no experience of torture, either of being tortured myself or, I hope, of torturing someone or something other than myself. But I may have tortured, under another name no doubt. But in order to determine this we would have to ask the person or animal which had felt tortured by me. I'm not really capable of answering that question objectively. As when someone from overseas asks me if Australia is still racist, I say, "I don't feel it, I'm part of the ruling culture, you will need to ask an Aborigine or a Chinese."

Does the torturer have to know what he or she is doing by the name torture in order to be committing an evil act? Skinner's students went on administering increasingly agonising electric shocks to their fellow students in the name of science even after some of the students had screamed and passed out a number of times. The torturers in that case saw themselves as members of a team engaged on a difficult and demanding behavioural experiment, without realising it was their own behaviour that was being scrutinised. Some people would say they had been brainwashed. But we are all brainwashed. We believe in our own realities. Can we say they were doing evil? Or being assiduous in the pursuit of truth? Jacob Rosenberg says truth is always sad. Our illusions concerning good and evil are deep and obscure and impossible to separate from the hypnotic realities of our situation; they are, I believe, subjective. We have to ask the other how we behave. That's why it's so easy, I believe, for us to judge the behaviour of others.

But the question, *Will you do evil with me by letting me do evil in your name?* is so direct. It is Miltonic and Dantesque and approximates the voice of the Satanic in our real public life. There is nowhere for us to hide from such a question. *How can people even ask such things? What is the world coming to, for goodness' sake?* It is, as Gaita shockingly points out to us, so new, so unexpected, so direct, and its implications so profound that we really can't see them all yet. It isn't, I imagine, whether this question asked in such a way will actually increase the practice of torture, but that it will corrupt us in ways that we have not been corrupt before. I hope I'm not misreading Gaita in this. He has opened this discussion with such force that I'm sure I'm still confused about a lot of things. I feel very grateful to him for not offering us a simplified address, and for offering us the question in all its complexity, its endless ambiguities and deep variations of tone and areas of shadow and shadows of shadows, cast and reflected and uplit from other structures that could easily confuse the mind. Wonderful! I couldn't help thinking of Plato's cave and the play of shadows on the walls. And that he maintained through this a calm sense of clarity and order in his prose amazed me. It is what the best philosophers have always done: to speak to the non-professional with clarity about complex moral questions on which they themselves have yet to reach a final position. Plato, and in more recent time Georges Bataille.

Alex Miller

Raimond Gaita

For different reasons, Paul Kelly, Paul Bongiorno and Mungo MacCallum think I don't understand Australian politics and that a disabling moral squint distorts my perception of the relations between morality and politics more generally.

Kelly rightly says that truthfulness or morally good intentions in politics will not redeem incompetence that causes much suffering, that in politics things are done that would not be permitted in private life, that in politics trust is tied irrevocably to outcomes, and that "political judgements ... are imprecise and uncertain and often made in the face of uncertainty as to the facts and the truth". These are the platitudes of elementary political literacy. In more than one place in my essay I indicate my agreement with them. But – it should be obvious – the fact that "political judgements ... are imprecise and uncertain" does not mean that there is no such thing as culpably muddying the waters and that when it is done intentionally it often counts as mendacity. Nor does the "irrevocable" connection between trust and consequences obviate the need to distinguish believing that someone will deliver the goods because one trusts him from believing that he will merely because one has grounds (usually his track record) to predict it. Kelly keeps saying that trust is a more complex notion than truthfulness, and it is, but neither in his column that I discuss in my essay, nor in his reply, does he (or Bongiorno who says rightly that there are degrees of trust) say anything that undermines my suggestion that the voters were not fooled when John Howard laid claim to their trust.

Kelly complains that I provide no evidence that Howard is "pervasively" and "systematically" mendacious. One reason I don't provide evidence to support such a claim is that I don't make it. The closest I come to it is in my opening paragraph when I say that Howard tried to distract the voters' attention from mounting evidence that he had been systematically mendacious. At other times the phrases are attributed to others, real or imagined. I don't want to make too much of this because in fact I believe that Howard *was* systematically mendacious, but it is not a small matter that I was careful to avoid saying it and that Kelly reads me too carelessly to notice.

Breach of Trust assumes that Howard was mendacious sufficiently often and on matters sufficiently important for people reasonably to believe that he should have been held to account more severely than he was by the electorate and by much of the media. I believe, though I do not say so, that he should have been voted out of office, but I am careful to acknowledge that nothing substantial can be inferred about the attitude to truth in politics, reconciliation, the refugees or the invasion of Iraq from the fact that so many people thought differently.

Kelly shows no corresponding caution in his verdict on those who argued that Howard should go because they believed that he had been pervasively mendacious about some of the most important matters of recent Australian politics. They expressed, he says, a "judgement devoid of any balance". This then is the situation: Australians whom Kelly acknowledges to be influential and many in number deplore a government that administers a cruel detention policy which has left some children for years behind razor wire, watching adults go mad and suffering forms of mental illness themselves; a government that deliberately sows confusion about the relations between symbolic and practical reconciliation (delivering incidentally almost nothing on practical reconciliation); a government that takes the country to a war which no one could seriously call one of last resort, all the while recklessly muddying the waters about the reason why it went to war. You don't have to agree with that description of the government, and, if you do, you don't have to believe that it should have been voted out of office. But can you say that those who believed that it should have been show no balance in their political judgement? *No balance at all* because they are intoxicated by a politically stupid and dangerous moralism? Only if you have contempt for them.

I hoped that it would be evident to readers that *Breach of Trust* does not even try to provide evidence for its assumption about the nature and seriousness of the many forms of Howard's mendacity. One kind of essay might have set out to provide such evidence. Another kind might have provided definitions of the different kinds of mendacity and arguments about which were permissible. My essay attempts, instead, to try to understand the kinds of importance that truth and truthfulness can have in politics. It did not seek to offer definitions or moral guidance, but sought instead to delineate the conceptual space in which we might understand more clearly what, often inchoately, informs our thoughts about politics. It focused on our thoughts about patriotism, on judgements about what should be included in a decent conception of the national interest and what we can do to protect it, on how one might understand the suspicion, voiced so often, that there is a deep and irreconcilable conflict between morality and politics, and how all this bears on our responses to the dangerous world we now live in.

Why, Kelly and Bongiorno ask, did so many people vote for Howard if he is so evidently the reprobate character I and others believe him to be? I don't know (though of course I have read much of the speculation about this), but, as I said earlier, I see no reason to believe that they voted for him because they trusted him. I emphasised the degree to which Howard and many of his supporters in the intelligentsia have entangled what should not be controversial in a politically literate and decent community with what is properly controversial – entangling, for example, the wicked belief that it is justifiable to hold children behind razor wire as part of a deterrent to other asylum seekers with the many difficulties anyone will encounter when they think seriously about refugee and immigration policies.

In the case of Iraq, people were encouraged to believe that reasons – none of which would be morally sufficient in themselves to justify invasion – became morally sufficient when taken together. Sometimes reasons add up in that way, but it is not always so and seldom do a number of bad reasons add up to a good one. Part of my argument, developed more fully in my contribution to *Why the War Was Wrong*, concludes that you cannot just put together fears about Saddam's alleged possession of weapons of mass destruction, the humanitarian case for his overthrow and the hopes for a reconstructed Middle East, and achieve sufficient a reason to go to war. To be sure the matter is arguable and decent people will disagree. But to acknowledge even that is to deprive the question of why so many voted for Howard of nearly all the rhetorical force with which Kelly, and to a lesser extent Bongiorno, tried to invest it.

Kelly and Bongiorno think that "the Australian people" (as Kelly calls them, presumably excluding moralists, absolutists and others who lack all political balance) knew that the real reason we went to war was not to disarm Saddam, whom they knew to be of no danger to us, but to strengthen our alliance with America. Kelly gives an elaborate account, unsupported by any evidence, of how the collective Australian mind reasoned about this. If he is right, most Australians who voted for Howard cared little for the fact that the reasons we went to war were not the reasons we were given and therefore cared little for the fact that in a democracy the reasons for which a government takes its citizens to war should be the reasons it has given them. (Kelly says, extraordinarily, that Howard merely "fudged" the fact that the real reason we went to war was "because of the US alliance".) From Kelly's perspective, this insouciance on the part of the electorate about the gap between what a government actually says, and what those who are possessed of sufficient political acumen can infer that it means, is a sign of realism and healthy scepticism. In a predecessor essay in *Griffith Review*, I wrote: "Howard's cynical pact with the electorate – he is mendacious and much of the electorate lets it pass for so long as its material and security interests are satisfied – has undermined the possibility for Australians to celebrate lucidly the love of country that he so often professes to feel and to have promoted." The first part of that comes close to Kelly's assessment of how ordinary Australians responded to Howard's changing reasons about why we invaded Iraq, though it judges that response differently. In *Breach of Trust* I repented of attributing such cynicism to the people who voted for Howard.

Kelly says that in the column he wrote for the *Australian*, he did not justify Howard's mendacity (such as it was) about when he knew that no children had been thrown overboard. He was concerned, he says, only to place such mendacity in its historical context and to show that more often than not it arose from preceding failures of policy. But Kelly did not just say that people who thought Howard was more mendacious than other prime ministers were mistaken, and that they were naive if they thought that any prime minister would have acted differently from Howard (assuming Howard lied) on the eve of an election. Nor did he just urge them to be more attentive to the kinds of failures in policy that often tempted prime ministers to one or other form of mendacity. When he called them moralists, intending all that word's pejorative connotations, implied they were absolutists about truth in politics and that they had yielded to the illusion that politics is a "morality contest", he denied Howard's critics the standards in whose light his mendacity could seriously be criticised. I'll let readers judge how much that differs from a justification.

It comes as no surprise that Mungo MacCallum offers different reasons for why Australians voted for Howard in such large numbers. Clearly he exaggerates when he says that "Howard's actions makes it clear that … the acquisition and retention of power transcend all ethical considerations" because for him, as for many politicians, "l'état est moi." But the essence of his point, as I understand it, is that when politicians radically identify the national interest with their own interest in staying in office, then certain kinds of moral judgements lapse because concepts – particularly those that depend on the attribution of particular intentions – cease to apply. If, as he puts it, a leader comes to think that he is the state, then we must judge him differently from someone who pursues power, perhaps ruthlessly, but for reasons other than his own advancement. When I described the people of central Victoria, as I knew them in the '50s, I suggested that they had a worldly but entirely uncorrupted conception of the pleasure that it is legitimate to take in the exercise of power, but that they also knew well enough how often power "goes to one's head". It's an interesting phrase and expresses a thought different from the thought that power often corrupts, because it implies that one has, in one of the many ways it is possible to do so, lost contact with reality. Some of this I tried to capture when I said that for a time New Labour's sophisticated spin made it difficult for the British to see the ground onto which they could plant their feet and from where they could soberly judge their government. I also alluded briefly to the ways in which the members of the Christian triumvirate had, in their different ways, become victims of their own spin. That means we have to be careful in the ways we describe things, alert to the possibility that the concepts we are first inclined to use may no longer apply. But it does not mean that we must acknowledge a "new ethical reality", not, at any rate, if that means that we are in need of new ethical concepts.

It is a big fact about politics as we know it that policies are often judged retrospectively in the light of their consequences. Supporters of the war in Iraq are already imagining the historical narratives that will present the invasion as the beginning of the growth of democracies throughout the Middle East. If that happens, William Kristol and Robert Kagan, two leading American neo-conservative theorists, wrote (in an article reprinted in the *Australian* on 8 February), no one will deserve more credit than George W. Bush.

If democracy flourishes in Iraq, Kristol and Kagan are right to think that Bush will be given the credit for it. If he is denied it, it will not be because of serious moral reservations, but because there will be disputes about what consequences can be attributed to him and about how much he knew what he was doing. That is often how we read history. The people who were sacrificed are mostly forgotten. Whatever is to be said for adopting that perspective on our political history (people are increasingly resistant to it), we should not adopt it in the present, at the moments of deliberation and decision. If we do, we are likely to become intoxicated by the image of ourselves as actors in a grand historical narrative. Much more than military escapades in pursuit of financial objectives, political action that springs from such motives tends to be ruthlessly indifferent to its human costs. Why should doers of historical grand deeds, agents of massive geo-political change, stoop to count corpses?

This much should be taken on board by people who take morally seriously the idea that war should always be a last resort because each human life is infinitely precious: it is much more interesting and (as Nietzsche saw plainly and ruthlessly) much more invigorating to think of politics as grand historical action than it is to remind people (oneself very much included) of the human costs of such adventures. Indeed there is nothing *interesting* about the claim that the destruction of each life is the destruction of a miracle, nothing about it that excites the mind and, except in saints, little to impel one to action. That, I assume, is why, before the invasion and after, the reminder that through the agency of the coalition we had killed tens of thousands of Iraqis was treated, often with urbane condescension, as a tedious interruption of the excitement of geo-political action, and in the case of the intelligentsia, especially journalists, of endless geo-political speculation.

Grant therefore for the sake of argument that Bush invaded Iraq to liberate the Iraqis and to help them and others in the Middle East to establish democratic governments. These are noble ends. Many people recognised that even when they could not morally support the means to their achievement. (God only knows why Kelly describes many of them as having "marched for the moral cause of keeping the Iraqi people enslaved"!) Why, then, should anyone who believes the invasion of Iraq was unjust, aware from the beginning what its good consequences might be, now believe that the realisation of some of those consequences "help[s] the moral legitimacy of George Bush's position"?

When people say, aggressively or triumphantly, to opponents of the war that they must remember that Saddam would still be in power if they had had their way, and that millions of Iraqis would not have had the opportunity to vote in the recent elections, they seem to want to deny opponents of the war the right to be glad of such good consequences. But why should we not hope fervently for a democratic Iraq and be joyful if it should come to pass? If that is all Kelly means when he says that for an opponent of the war, good consequences can "redeem" the injustice of it, then I have no quarrel with him. But I cannot see that it lessens the injustice of it, and for that reason I cannot see why people who believed it to be unjust but who are glad of its good consequences should have those consequences aggressively thrown in their faces.

Paul Bongiorno says, "Surely we have to accept the existence of a transnational phenomenon dedicated to the destruction of the Western culture of which we are a part." Whatever one makes of that "surely", as things stand it is (as the British Law Lords recently noticed) our responses to terrorism rather than terrorism that threatens the values we hold dear. Terrorists threaten only our lives. That of course is no small matter, but when Bongiorno suggests that my acknowledgement that politicians will always do evil when it is necessary for the defence of community should at least soften my hostility to the Christian triumvirate, he ignores entirely the significance of the distinction between the obligation on politicians to protect the lives of their citizens and the obligation on them to protect what I sometimes call the "very conditions of human communality". Bongiorno appears to argue, in effect, that our participation in the invasion was a form of self-defence because it was intended to strengthen the alliance with America, an alliance that we need if we are to defend ourselves against "al-Qaeda and its fellow travellers". Unholy alliances may be truly enough described as a form of self-defence, but I do not see how our participation in an unjust war becomes a just act of self-defence because we have done it to secure the protection of a powerful ally. Perhaps it is because he knows this is what anyone who stays within coo-ee of the traditional doctrine of just war will say, that Bongiorno believes we need a "different paradigm" to think about the war against terror. I take him to mean that we need to revise our beliefs in the light of radically new circumstances, or perhaps alter some fundamental moral concepts. But Bongiorno gives us no reason to believe this. Terrorism of the kind we are facing may be relatively new, but the problem it presents us with is very old: what are we prepared to do to protect ourselves and those who are dependent on us.

If politicians were to accept views such as mine, Kelly argues, they would be incapable of prosecuting the war on terror effectively. He thinks that partly because he seems, entirely without justification and indeed against the grain of my discussion, to take me for a kind of pacifist, and partly, perhaps, because he has noted my argument that a politician who refuses to torture for the sake of saving even the lives of thousands of his citizens has not failed in his distinctive political obligations. I know, of course, that he will not agree with that, and I readily acknowledge my argument for it to be the most controversial part of the essay. But my discussion of it and the distinctions that I draw to support it can hardly be described as the expression of a moral view that is simplistic in the extreme. Nor can the tone of it justly be described as one in which I betray my desire to impose a morality on politicians or anyone else. Even less can it support his claim that I fail to understand "the compact of democratic governance … [that] governments have a responsibility to govern and that often requires inflicting hurt upon people (higher taxes, lower benefits) that would be unacceptable in the moral relations between two individuals".

*

Natasha Cica expresses much of what I was trying to do in *Breach of Trust* when she elaborates the false disjunctions that are so often pressed on us in these coarsened days of cultural combat. After brooding for some time about why Kelly felt the need to remind me of the platitudes I enumerated earlier, about why he took me for some kind of pacifist, about why he believed that I wanted to "impose" on politicians moral views that are "simplistic in the extreme", I was much heartened that neither she nor Alex Miller saw over-simplification in what I had written, nor did they find in its tone — in its *many* tones as Miller has rightly pointed out — a desire to impose moral positions on anyone. Focusing as he does on my discussion of torture, Miller sees clearly that I have no simple moral maxim (Kant's or anyone else's) which I use as a test for political conduct. If I had, I would not have relied as much as I did on Primo Levi's story from *If This Is a Man*, nor would I have developed my argument in such a personal form. "I speak for myself," I often remind my readers.

Miller asks profound questions about what we may learn about ourselves when we face honestly the reasons why we are now discussing whether the war on terror has given us grounds to approve limited forms of torture and there-fore reason to modify the international law which prohibits torture in all circumstances. The argument is that when the chips are down, when we soberly contemplate the human cost of adhering to international law on the prohibition on torture, then we will realise that in our hearts we did not believe the prohi-bition should be exceptionless. This, I have claimed, is an argument we must reluctantly face. I am pessimistic about the outcome. After we have had our pub-lic debate, we will, I think, support torture, but I do not think this because I have a low opinion of human nature. Or perhaps more accurately, reasons that focus on the dark side of our nature are not the ones which I wanted to explore in my essay. The part of our tradition that could support an exceptionless ban on tor-ture for other than prudential reasons has always been sublime, and humanity was perhaps at the best of times always "clinging in recollection to wonders it had seen" (to use Plato's beautiful expression to describe the waxing and waning of a certain kind of moral sensibility) — wonders that had compelled some people to testify that all human beings are precious, that all evil-doers are owed the kind of respect that Kant called unconditional, and that no human being should be treated like filth.

Our estrangement from that part of our tradition is what makes me pessimistic about our capacity to resist the increasing pressures on us to consent to the torture of terrorists so that we and our children will be safe. Just as there have always been people who will say that war is always a filthy business in order to undermine the idea that standards of justice and respect for the enemy apply in even the fiercest war, so people are now saying that of course torture is always a terrible thing, but the world is a very imperfect place. Such people like pacifists because they can safely express their moral admiration for them and for their sincerity without feeling in the slightest challenged by them. When such people say that war or torture are terrible, they do not mean that they are *morally* terrible. They mean something deliberately vague because it enables them to undermine any clear sense of the distinction between what is psychologically traumatic and what is morally terrible – to undermine any clear sense of that distinction as it would inform strict standards of decency even when we are fighting desperately for our lives.

There are two kinds of points to be made about realism. One depends on an assessment of human nature, of what people are capable of and how events will turn out. One might be pessimistic about that while describing political conduct in terms of standards that are seldom met, or that have to some degree been forgotten, or which depends on concepts on which we have an ever-diminishing grasp. So much is conveyed in the idea that politicians are not a moral bunch, but the least interesting aspects of that idea focus on their personal failings or the moral failings of human beings generally. If, as Natasha Cica suggests, politicians now often lack character, then that is at least in part because the concept of character – and with it the concept of honour – plays such an inchoate role in modern life. That takes me to the second kind of point that one can make about realism.

Politics, the cliché goes, is the art of the possible, constrained by realities. But among "the possible" are moral possibilities, and among the constraining realities there are moral realities. Some possibilities are open only when one has a serious concept of a political *vocation*; some are open only when one thinks of the national interest as in part constituted by our interest in being just and in being able to love our country without shame; some are open only when one distinguishes a politician's obligation to protect lives of citizens from her obligation to protect the conditions under which community may survive into the future, or when one does not set symbolic reconciliation in opposition to practical reconciliation.

But – and this is a big "but" and it leads me to enter a serious qualification on Cica's development of what I had to say about character in politics – my interest was not primarily in the kind of character that is desirable in a politician. I wanted instead to delineate the conceptual space in which one could speak seriously of, among other things, political honour. And unlike Max Weber who was concerned in his classic essay "Politics as a Vocation" to draw a portrait of what kind of man could "lay his hands on the wheels of history", I was more concerned to discuss what we, as citizens, could require of our governments as an exercise of their distinctive political responsibility, and what we should do to prevent love of country degenerating into jingoism. In this connection I wanted to argue that much of our sense of a conflict between morality and politics is informed by a sense that moral value does not necessarily override all other value for a morally serious person. I expressed this by saying that a politician must sometimes, understanding the obligations of her vocation, do what morally she must not do. To put it another way, politics is a realm *sui generis*. Acknowledgement of that informs the character of a politician's responsiveness to the incommensurable imperatives of her vocation, and of our understanding of what we can expect and require of her.

It frightens me to write in this way about politics because I sometimes fear that in characterising a politician's answerability to conflicting imperatives – one moral, the other political – as tragic, I will be seen to be justifying – perhaps encouraging – evil to be done. I have tried to do the opposite – to rescue this perception from romanticism of a kind found (in my judgement) in, for example, Albert Camus's *The Rebel* and in some of the writings on just war of the modern American philosopher Michael Walzer.

To many it will sound like weaselling, I know, but I do not offer a *justification* for the evil that politicians must sometimes do. When someone says that she must do such and such, and the necessity she expresses is not physical, psychological or social compulsion but the expression of a value that goes deep in her, then she is not necessarily trying to justify what she says she must do. That is one of the important differences between "must" and "ought" in these contexts. Even in our most famous expression of such necessity, "Here I stand. I can do no other," Luther was not then justifying what he was doing, though, of course, he would offer plenty of justifications for his condemnations of the Church, condemnations which informed his sense that he had to act as he did. A political leader who says she cannot do evil although the life of the community really is at stake (usually politicians do evil before that, of course – as we have done, if Kelly and Bongiorno are right to say that we invaded Iraq to increase the chances that America will defend us when we need it) may be criticised for failing as a politician, but that just means that she failed to rise to one of the conflicting and incommensurable imperative that claimed her. If she says that morally she cannot do the evil that her political vocation now requires of her even though that will place the community in mortal danger, she need not – if she is lucid, she will not – imply that she has come clear-sightedly to the realisation that morality has a greater claim, not just on her, but period.

Instead of offering a justification, I tried to characterise the nature of the values in which the political imperative is rooted. I tried to explain why obedience to it can be seen (again without an attempt to justify it) as an expression of loyalty, not just to this or that community, but to the conditions of communality. Why to the conditions of communality? Because politicians know that politics is essentially and distinctively committed to the future, to the survival into the future, not just of people, but of peoples. They are required to try to ensure that, as Hannah Arendt put it, "men, not man inhabit the earth," to ensure, that is to say, the conditions for human plurality persist. But, as I said, it frightens me that even someone who does not see in this an attempt to justify the evil that politicians must sometimes do might instead see it in the seductive light of an ersatz sense of the tragic. Such a light fails to display the full terror of the dilemma politicians face if one horn of that dilemma is constituted for them by a full understanding of why it is better to suffer evil than to do it.

Natasha Cica directly, and Alex Miller more indirectly, speak of hope and of goodness. Miller says that he has always been reluctant to acknowledge the reality of evil. Many people don't like the word "evil". Understandably but mistakenly they take it to be the expression of moral simple-mindedness and of an unsavoury disposition to demonise wrong-doers. I take the concept seriously, as expressing a distinctive moral category, but one which we will distort unless we think of evil as properly visible to us only in the (often indirect) light of the good. To put the point more concretely: we have a serious use for the concept of evil only, I believe, when we have a sense of the inalienable preciousness of every human being, when, as I put it earlier, we look upon each life as a miracle. But that sense has been granted us, I think, not by abstract doctrine, theological or philosophical, but by what the love of saints has revealed to us about human beings. Charles's behaviour, as Primo Levi recounts it, is an example of such love. There are many others. In many ways we in the West have tried to make the fruits of that love tractable to reason, and Kant's formulation – that we must never treat another human being merely as a means to our ends but as an end in herself – is an example of such an attempt. Here is not the place for me to try to explain why I believe those attempts have failed, except to say that in failing to make such love and what it has taught us more tractable to reason, we have failed to provide just the kind of test that Kelly thinks I apply, and with it the kind of justification someone seeks when he asks: Which is justified – to follow the political or the moral imperative in cases of tragic conflict?

Be that as it may. The goodness that has been shown to us in the example of saintly men and women throughout our history is there for us to see, if we are directed to it. For that reason despair can never be a necessity for someone who clear-sightedly sees the terrible suffering and evil in the world. No one will ever be justified in saying, "How could anyone but a fool fail to see that this world is not worth living in, not worth our loyalty, not worth teaching our children to love?"

To develop that point further in response to Cica's and Miller's letters would require me to write another *Quarterly Essay*, longer perhaps than the one I have written. For that reason I have for the most part limited myself to the easier task of responding to my critics.

Raimond Gaita

Paul Bongiorno is Network 10's Parliament House bureau chief in Canberra. He has been the presenter of the national political program *Meet the Press* since 1996.

Natasha Cica is a visiting fellow at the Gilbert + Tobin Centre of Public Law at the University of New South Wales. She was the founding editor of NewMatilda.com and has worked as an adviser to a number of federal parliamentarians.

Raimond Gaita is Professor of Moral Philosophy at King's College, University of London and Professor of Philosophy at the Australian Catholic University. His books include the award-winning *Romulus, My Father, Good and Evil: An Absolute Conception, A Common Humanity, The Philosopher's Dog* and *Why the War Was Wrong* (as editor and contributor).

John Hirst is a widely respected historian and social commentator. Reader in History at La Trobe University, he is the author of several books, including *Convict Society and Its Enemies, The Sentimental Nation* and *Australia's Democracy*, as well as many commentaries for leading Australian newspapers and journals. John Hirst has also had a number of influential appointments. He was a member of the Prime Minister's Republic Advisory Committee and the chair of the Commonwealth Civics Education Group. He is currently a member of the Film Australia Board and the council of the National Museum.

Paul Kelly is the Editor-at-Large of the *Australian*. Among his books are *The End of Certainty, Paradise Divided* and *100 Years: The Australian Story*.

Mungo MacCallum's books include *Run, Johnny, Run, How To Be a Megalomaniac* and *Mungo: The Man Who Laughs*. His Quarterly Essay, *Girt by Sea: Australia, the Refugees and the Politics of Fear*, was published in 2002.

Alex Miller's novels include *The Ancestor Game, Conditions of Faith* and *Journey to the Stone Country*. His new novel, *Prochownik's Dream*, will be published later this year.

QUARTERLY ESSAY

POST OR FAX TO: Quarterly Essay
Reply Paid 79448
Melbourne VIC 3000
T: 61 3 9654 2000 F: 61 3 9654 2290
E: quarterlyessay@blackincbooks.com

SUBSCRIPTIONS Receive a discount and never miss an issue. Mailed direct to your door.

1 year subscription (4 issues): $49 a year within Australia incl. GST (Institutional subs. $59). Outside Australia $79. All prices include postage and handling.

2 year subscription (8 issues): $95 a year within Australia incl. GST (Institutional subs $115). Outside Australia $155. All prices include postage and handling.

BACK ISSUES Please add $2.50 postage and handling to your order (or $8.00 for overseas orders).

☐ **Issue 1** ($9.95) Robert Manne *In Denial: The Stolen Generations and the Right*
☐ **Issue 2** ($9.95) John Birmingham *Appeasing Jakarta: Australia's Complicity in the East Timor Tragedy*
☐ **Issue 3** ($9.95) Guy Rundle *The Opportunist: John Howard and the Triumph of Reaction*
☐ **Issue 4** ($9.95) Don Watson *Rabbit Syndrome: Australia and America*
☐ **Issue 5** ($11.95) Mungo MacCallum *Girt by Sea: Australia, the Refugees and the Politics of Fear*
☐ **Issue 6** ($11.95) John Button *Beyond Belief: What Future for Labor?*
☐ **Issue 7** ($11.95) John Martinkus *Paradise Betrayed: West Papua's Struggle for Independence*
☐ **Issue 8** ($11.95) Amanda Lohrey *Groundswell: The Rise of the Greens*
☐ **Issue 9** ($11.95) Tim Flannery *Beautiful Lies: Population and Environment in Australia*
☐ **Issue 10** ($12.95) Gideon Haigh *Bad Company: The Cult of the CEO*
☐ **Issue 11** ($12.95) Germaine Greer *Whitefella Jump Up: The Shortest Way to Nationhood*
☐ **Issue 12** ($12.95) David Malouf *Made in England: Australia's British Inheritance*
☐ **Issue 13** ($12.95) Robert Manne with David Corlett *Sending Them Home: Refugees and the New Politics of Indifference*
☐ **Issue 14** ($13.95) Paul McGeough *Mission Impossible: The Sheikhs, the US and the Future of Iraq*
☐ **Issue 15** ($13.95) Margaret Simons *Latham's World: The New Politics of the Outsiders*
☐ **Issue 16** ($13.95) Raimond Gaita *Breach of Trust: Truth, Morality and Politics*

PAYMENT DETAILS I enclose a cheque/money order made out to Schwartz Publishing Pty Ltd. Please debit my credit card (Mastercard, Visa or Bankcard accepted).

Card No. ☐☐☐☐ ☐☐☐☐ ☐☐☐☐ ☐☐☐☐

Expiry date   /   Amount $

Cardholder's name

Signature

Name

Address

Email

Subscribe online at **www.quarterlyessay.com**

www.ingramcontent.com/pod-product-compliance
Lightning Source LLC
Chambersburg PA
CBHW080608090426
42735CB00017B/3362